From the Block to the Bank

How to Make the Most of Your Circumstance to Maximize Your Full Potential

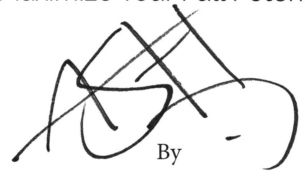

By

Ash Cash

DISCLAIMER

The advice contained in this material might not be suitable for everyone. The author designed the information to present his opinion about the subject matter. The reader must carefully investigate all aspects of any business decision before committing to him or herself. The author obtained the information contained herein from sources he believes to be reliable and from his own personal experience, but he neither implies nor intends any guarantee of accuracy. The author is not in the business of giving legal, accounting, or any other type of professional advice. Should the reader need such advice, he or she must seek services from a competent professional. The author particularly disclaims any liability, loss, or risk taken by individuals who directly or indirectly act on the information contained herein. The author believes the advice presented here is sound, but readers cannot hold him responsible for either the actions they take or the risk taken by individuals who directly or indirectly act on the information contained herein.

Published by 1BrickPublishing
Printed in the United States
Copyright © 2021 by Ash'Cash
ISBN 978-1949303278

DEDICATION

This book is dedicated to anyone who has ever been told that they wouldn't amount to anything. To those who were born to be great but because of their surroundings they thought the opposite. You are made in the image and likeness of the most high which makes you g.o.d = Greatness On Display! Today is the day you accept and walk into your GREATNESS!!!!

DEDICATION REQUEST

Please pass a copy of this book to anyone you care about who needs some inspiration, motivation and practical tips on how to maximize their full potential.

ACKNOWLEDGEMENT

I want to thank the Village of Harlem and every village across the world that takes responsibility whether directly or indirectly for the villagers. To the Gangster, the Gentleman, the number runners, the Street vendors, the trappers, the Shooters, the Entrepreneurs, the Hoopers, the basketball coaches, the teachers, the Scholars, the 9to5ers, the City workers, the scammers, the boosters, the Goons, the stick-up kids, the churches, the Gods, the Earths, the Pastors, The Ushers, the Deacons, the Nation, the Akhi's, The Imams, The 5%ers, the Israelites, the Pimps, the Gold diggers & Goal Hitters, the Dope fiends, the Crackheads, the Whinos, Papi and Habib, to the Oyeah's on Broadway, the Dons, the Divas, the MC's, the Battle rappers, the Poets, the Hoteps, the Orishas, the Ancestors! The fallen Soldiers and the Homies behind the wall! To every aspect of the hood that has made me who I am today and forever. Thank you

CONTENTS

Ash Cash Deposit Ticket

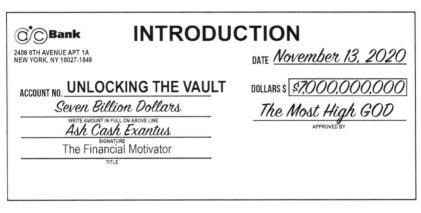

⊙Bank

2406 8TH AVENUE APT 1A
NEW YORK, NY 10027-1849

INTRODUCTION

DATE *November 13, 2020*

ACCOUNT NO. **UNLOCKING THE VAULT**

DOLLARS $ *$7,000,000,000*

Seven Billion Dollars

The Most High GOD

WRITE AMOUNT IN FULL ON ABOVE LINE

APPROVED BY

Ash Cash Exantus

SIGNATURE

The Financial Motivator

TITLE

⊙ ASH CASH EXANTUS

INTRODUCTION – UNLOCKING THE VAULT

You ain't sh*t, You ain't never gone be sh*t your mama ain't sh*t, Your family ain't sh*t, Your life doesn't mean sh*t! You're a waste of air! Why were you even born? These are the messages that repeatedly played in my head for most of my life coming up. I was born to an immigrant mother who spoke no English; my father didn't want me, my brother didn't like me, and my sister beat me up. My neighborhood was filled with crack and poverty, the church despised me, the schools thought I was dumb and wanted to put me in special ed, and my basketball coaches didn't think I was good enough. The cops wanted me in jail, the TV kept telling me I was better off dead, and the old ladies in the neighborhood agreed. I had to fight physically and mentally every day to simply survive; my very existence was a struggle, and I had nothing and no one to turn to for guidance.

My lack of guidance resulted in me becoming a product of my environment. I lost my virginity, saw a dead body, and almost lost my life by a train moving at 110 miles per hour, all before my 12th birthday. Shoot-outs and crew fights were so typical they became entertaining. I had seen grown men stripped naked, pistol-whipped, and begging for their lives. I never shot anyone but owned a few illegal guns, I never sold drugs but held the stash for my drug-dealing friends a few times. I tagged on walls, stole from stores, and had many encounters on Pebble Beach (IYKYK). My friends were in and out of jail, so on weekends instead of hooping or doing what teenagers do, I took long bus trips to correctional facilities where the visitors were violated and disrespected, the same and sometimes worse than the prisoners.

The first time I was kicked out of school was in the 1st grade, and it gradually became a trend. I was kicked out of the 5th and 9th Grade for fighting then expelled in the 10th grade for being in the wrong place at the wrong time, causing me to repeat the 10th Grade. When it was time to graduate from high school, my grades were so bad that the ONLY school that would accept me was my local community college.

Despite my childhood experience, today, I am The Greatest Money Mindset Coach on the Planet and One of the World's top Financial Educators. I am financially free and run multiple businesses with my wife, best friend, and the mother of my two children (all the same person). I am a Best-Selling author who has written over ten books, and I have positively affected millions of lives. I have been featured on most major media outlets worldwide, and I am regarded as the Financial Motivator because of my unmatched energy. I have created countless millionaires directly and indirectly and have helped thousands of families break the generational curse of poverty and create true financial freedom.

I earned an associate's degree in Finance and Investments and made the dean's list more than four times. I received a Bachelor's degree in Entrepreneurship Management from one of the top business schools in the country. As a banker, I was ranked 112 among more than 100,000 bankers, which put me in the top 1%. I was a Vice President at a global financial institution at the age of twenty-four, managed more than five branches for major banks controlling over $500 Million in Assets throughout my career, opened an $8MM branch from scratch, and became one of the youngest CEOs of a federally chartered bank at thirty-one. I have inspired and motivated thousands of people worldwide through my live events, interviews, and online videos that have been seen millions of times. When it's all said and done (In God's will), I will be an Emmy Award-winning television host and producer, and my show will attract millions of viewers and listeners. I will host a Globally Syndicated Radio Show and win countless awards for being at the forefront of self-improvement. I will sell millions of copies of my books, and all of my ventures will continue to provide jobs and entrepreneurial opportunities for millions of people.

The bible says, "write it down and make it plain," The Quran says, "Verily, all things have we created in (planned) proportion and measure." The Torah says, "Commit to the Lord whatever you do, and he will establish your plans.", The Law of Attraction says, "Thoughts become things with Action." This all means that the life you want to live starts with your plans, then you must have faith in those plans and do what you are guided to do to achieve those plans. My life didn't start to shift until I had a clear vision of where I wanted to go, and as I started believing in that vision, my life began to flourish.

As you can tell by my story, I am unique, but I am not special. No matter where you come from, what your background is, or your current circumstance, the life you are living RIGHT NOW is in direct proportion to what you believe. Growing up, I didn't believe that my life was worth much, so my life and actions reflected that. Once I realized my worth, I started to command more out of life, and life answered accordingly.

I wrote this book because I am in debt. I stand on the shoulders of those who came before me, those who believed in me, and those who selflessly poured into me. I owe everyone who never gave up on me, those who saw in me what I couldn't see in myself despite my ignorance and behavior.

This book serves as a memoir and self-help guide that teaches you how to maximize your FULL potential regardless of your circumstances. As someone that society and statistics wanted to label as a predator, menace, and threat to my community, this book allows me the opportunity to show the world that a person's perceived characterizations do not have to dictate their future. It serves as a guide to remind people that no matter what others say or think about them, they have infinite possibilities to tap into once they believe in their higher self.

My life is a gift from the most high, and gifts are meant to be unwrapped and given. In the bank, the vault is where all of the valuables are stored and secured. Our mind, experiences, and life story are all valuable, so metaphorically these things are your vault. It's time for me to unlock the vault and bless those who are ready to take their life to the next level.

This book is broken down into four transactions:

- Transaction #1 is the Account Analyst, which will give you a high-level account of the significant moments of my life.

- Transaction #2 is the Opening Deposit; this will give you an account of my story from the beginning to the present.

- Transaction #3 is the Cash Advance which comprises 40 lessons or principles that I learned and used to be where I am today and overcome ANY obstacle and a return on Investment on how you can implement what you learned in your life; This section will give you a blueprint.

- Transaction #4 is the Statement Audit, aka my receipts. I didn't want this book to be written solely from my recollection, so I wanted to know what the people closest to me think? In compiling this section, I wanted to make sure that I was removed from hearing or seeing the stories so that they remain authentic. With that said, some of the stories may contradict what I said or validate it. I'm not sure, but I wanted to give you all sides of the coin. Special shout out to Naadira Brown, who conducted the interviews; she was very adamant in making sure I didn't see or alter the responses in any way.

- Transaction #5 is Additional Deposit which is other books by Ash Cash and Ash Cash/Abundance Community Merch. If you are Greatness On Display or Believe that Abundance is Your Birthright then wear it on your head and/or your chest.

I hope you enjoy this book and if you do, please be sure to tell a friend, coworker, organization, and your social media followers. I intend to help as many people as possible recognize that abundance is their birthright, so I thank you in advance for helping me live out my purpose.

Ash Cash Deposit Ticket

Bank   **TRANSACTION #1**

2406 8TH AVENUE APT 1A
NEW YORK, NY 10027-1849

DATE *November 13, 2020*

ACCOUNT NO. **ACCOUNT ANALYSIS**

DOLLARS $ *$200,000,000*

Two hundred million dollars
WRITE AMOUNT IN FULL ON ABOVE LINE

The Most High GOD
APPROVED BY

Ash Cash Exantus
SIGNATURE

The Financial Motivator
TITLE

 ASH CASH EXANTUS

TRANSACTION #1
ACCOUNT ANALYSIS

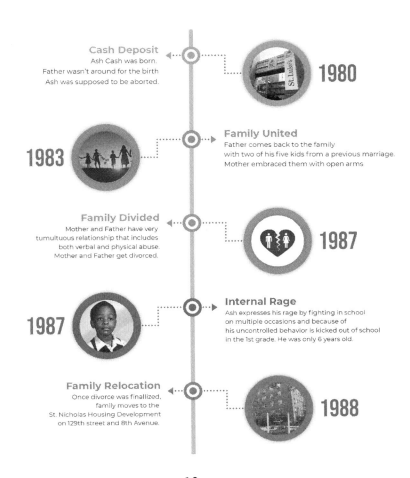

Cash Deposit
Ash Cash was born.
Father wasn't around for the birth
Ash was supposed to be aborted.

1980

1983

Family United
Father comes back to the family
with two of his five kids from a previous marriage.
Mother embraced them with open arms

Family Divided
Mother and Father have very
tumultuous relationship that includes
both verbal and physical abuse.
Mother and Father get divorced.

1987

1987

Internal Rage
Ash expresses his rage by fighting in school
on multiple occasions and because of
his uncontrolled behavior is kicked out of school
in the 1st grade. He was only 6 years old.

Family Relocation
Once divorce was finallized,
family moves to the
St. Nicholas Housing Development
on 129th street and 8th Avenue.

1988

From the Block to the Bank

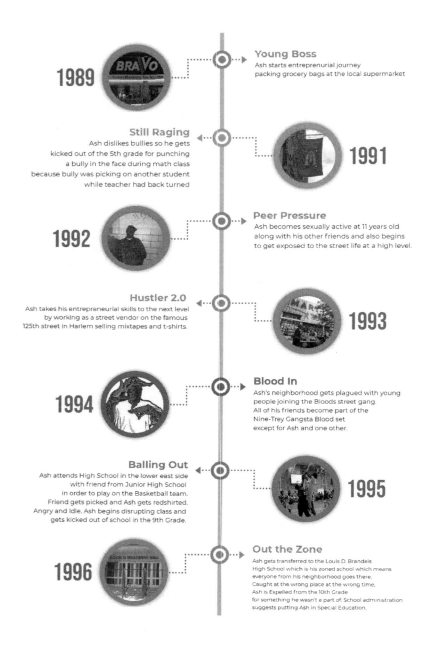

1989

Young Boss
Ash starts entreprenurial journey
packing grocery bags at the local supermarket

Still Raging
Ash dislikes bullies so he gets
kicked out of the 5th grade for punching
a bully in the face during math class
because bully was picking on another student
while teacher had back turned

1991

1992

Peer Pressure
Ash becomes sexually active at 11 years old
along with his other friends and also begins
to get exposed to the street life at a high level.

Hustler 2.0
Ash takes his entrepreneurial skills to the next level
by working as a street vendor on the famous
125th street in Harlem selling mixtapes and t-shirts.

1993

1994

Blood In
Ash's neighborhood gets plagued with young
people joining the Bloods street gang.
All of his friends become part of the
Nine-Trey Gangsta Blood set
except for Ash and one other.

Balling Out
Ash attends High School in the lower east side
with friend from Junior High School
in order to play on the Basketball team.
Friend gets picked and Ash gets redshirted.
Angry and Idle, Ash begins disrupting class and
gets kicked out of school in the 9th Grade.

1995

1996

Out the Zone
Ash gets transferred to the Louis D. Brandeis
High School which is his zoned school which means
everyone from his neighborhood goes there.
Caught at the wrong place at the wrong time,
Ash is Expelled from the 10th Grade
for something he wasn't a part of. School administration
suggests putting Ash in Special Education.

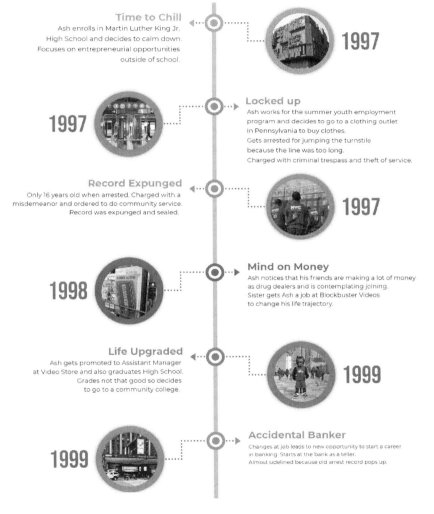

Time to Chill
Ash enrolls in Martin Luther King Jr. High School and decides to calm down. Focuses on entrepreneurial opportunities outside of school.

1997

1997

Locked up
Ash works for the summer youth employment program and decides to go to a clothing outlet in Pennsylvania to buy clothes.
Gets arrested for jumping the turnstile because the line was too long.
Charged with criminal trespass and theft of service.

Record Expunged
Only 16 years old when arrested. Charged with a misdemeanor and ordered to do community service. Record was expunged and sealed.

1997

1998

Mind on Money
Ash notices that his friends are making a lot of money as drug dealers and is contemplating joining. Sister gets Ash a job at Blockbuster Videos to change his life trajectory.

Life Upgraded
Ash gets promoted to Assistant Manager at Video Store and also graduates High School. Grades not that good so decides to go to a community college.

1999

1999

Accidental Banker
Changes at job leads to new opportunity to start a career in banking. Starts at the bank as a teller.
Almost sidelined because old arrest record pops up.

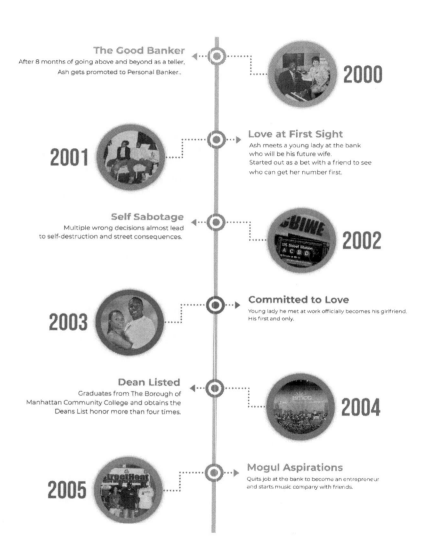

The Good Banker
After 8 months of going above and beyond as a teller,
Ash gets promoted to Personal Banker..

2000

2001

Love at First Sight
Ash meets a young lady at the bank
who will be his future wife.
Started out as a bet with a friend to see
who can get her number first.

Self Sabotage
Multiple wrong decisions almost lead
to self-destruction and street consequences.

2002

2003

Committed to Love
Young lady he met at work officially becomes his girlfriend.
His first and only.

Dean Listed
Graduates from The Borough of
Manhattan Community College and obtains the
Deans List honor more than four times.

2004

2005

Mogul Aspirations
Quits job at the bank to become an entrepreneur
and starts music company with friends.

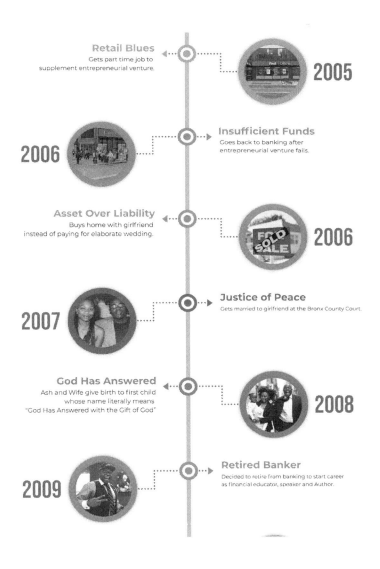

Retail Blues
Gets part time job to supplement entrepreneurial venture.

2005

2006

Insufficient Funds
Goes back to banking after entrepreneurial venture fails.

Asset Over Liability
Buys home with girlfriend instead of paying for elaborate wedding.

2006

2007

Justice of Peace
Gets married to girlfriend at the Bronx County Court.

God Has Answered
Ash and Wife give birth to first child whose name literally means "God Has Answered with the Gift of God"

2008

2009

Retired Banker
Decided to retire from banking to start career as financial educator, speaker and Author.

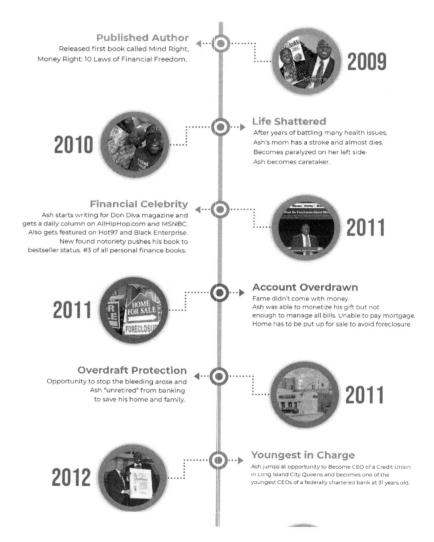

Published Author
Released first book called Mind Right,
Money Right: 10 Laws of Financial Freedom.

2009

2010

Life Shattered
After years of battling many health issues,
Ash's mom has a stroke and almost dies.
Becomes paralyzed on her left side.
Ash becomes caretaker.

Financial Celebrity
Ash starts writing for Don Diva magazine and
gets a daily column on AllHipHop.com and MSNBC.
Also gets featured on Hot97 and Black Enterprise.
New found notoriety pushes his book to
bestseller status. #3 of all personal finance books.

2011

2011

Account Overdrawn
Fame didn't come with money.
Ash was able to monetize his gift but not
enough to manage all bills. Unable to pay mortgage.
Home has to be put up for sale to avoid foreclosure.

Overdraft Protection
Opportunity to stop the bleeding arose and
Ash "unretired" from banking
to save his home and family.

2011

2012

Youngest in Charge
Ash jumps at opportunity to Become CEO of a Credit Union
in Long Island City Queens and becomes one of the
youngest CEOs of a federally chartered bank at 31 years old.

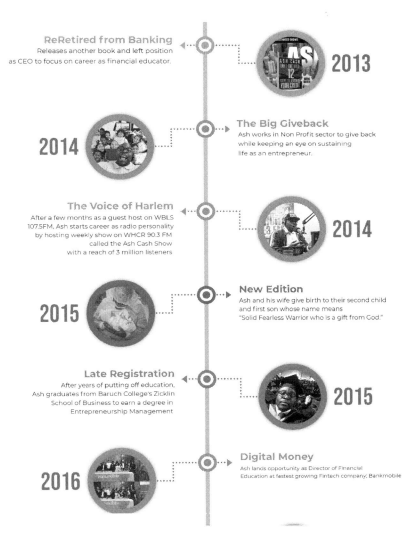

ReRetired from Banking
Releases another book and left position
as CEO to focus on career as financial educator.

2013

2014

The Big Giveback
Ash works in Non Profit sector to give back
while keeping an eye on sustaining
life as an entrepreneur.

The Voice of Harlem
After a few months as a guest host on WBLS
107.5FM, Ash starts career as radio personality
by hosting weekly show on WHCR 90.3 FM
called the Ash Cash Show
with a reach of 3 million listeners

2014

2015

New Edition
Ash and his wife give birth to their second child
and first son whose name means
"Solid Fearless Warrior who is a gift from God."

Late Registration
After years of putting off education,
Ash graduates from Baruch College's Zicklin
School of Business to earn a degree in
Entrepreneurship Management

2015

2016

Digital Money
Ash lands opportunity as Director of Financial
Education at fastest growing Fintech company; Bankmobile

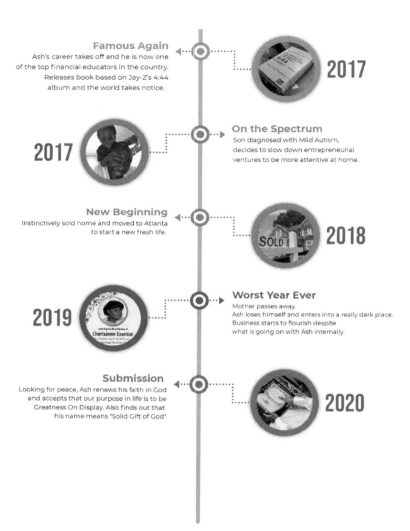

Famous Again
Ash's career takes off and he is now one
of the top financial educators in the country.
Releases book based on Jay-Z's 4:44
album and the world takes notice.

2017

2017

On the Spectrum
Son diagnosed with Mild Autism,
decides to slow down entrepreneurial
ventures to be more attentive at home.

New Beginning
Instinctively sold home and moved to Atlanta
to start a new fresh life.

2018

2019

Worst Year Ever
Mother passes away.
Ash loses himself and enters into a really dark place.
Business starts to flourish despite
what is going on with Ash internally.

Submission
Looking for peace, Ash renews his faith in God
and accepts that our purpose in life is to be
Greatness On Display. Also finds out that
his name means "Solid Gift of God"

2020

Ash Cash Deposit Ticket

ⓐ/ⓒBank 2406 8TH AVENUE APT 1A NEW YORK, NY 10027-1849	# TRANSACTION #2

DATE *November 13, 1980*

ACCOUNT NO. **OPENING DEPOSIT**

DOLLARS $ | *$0* |

Zero Dollars - You Owe Us
WRITE AMOUNT IN FULL ON ABOVE LINE

The Most High GOD
APPROVED BY

Ash Cash Exantus
SIGNATURE

The Financial Motivator
TITLE

TRANSACTION #2
OPENING DEPOSIT

I am the youngest of the three children my mother gave birth to, and I was told at a young age my dad had no desire for me to exist...

My story begins way before November 13, 1980, with the woman who was brave enough to give me a chance. My mother, aka Mommy, was born Cherisanne Nelson in Jacmel, Haiti, in a town dubbed the "City of Light," because it was the first in the Caribbean to have electricity. She was the 10th of 12 children.

Mommy attended the Siloé School in Jacmel, where she received her brevet diploma (diplôme national du brevet or DNB), an assessment, and a certificate acknowledging that you have the knowledge and skills required at the end of middle school to move on to the next level.

To provide financial support for her very large family, instead of attending high school, she opted to attend a trade school where she learned the creativity and technical skills needed to become a professional seamstress.

This skill would earn her the opportunity to work with many wealthy families in Haiti, which ultimately provided her the first trip to America in 1968 when she received a working Visa to tailor clothes for one of the families.

With her Visa, she would go back and forth between Haiti and America but realized that the opportunities in America were vast and she could be of better assistance to her loved ones if she stayed. In 1970 she officially made America her home and gave birth to her first son Daniel in 1972. In 1977 she married Wesner Exantus and later gave birth to her second child Roz.

Legend has it that in 1979 she became pregnant again, but due to pressure from her husband (my father), she decided not to proceed with the pregnancy. The following year, In 1980, she got pregnant again, and just like before, there was mounting pressure to terminate the pregnancy, but something inside of her told her to keep the baby (Pun intended). On November 13, 1980, at approximately 7:45 am in the St. Luke's Hospital in Harlem, NY, she gave birth to me without my dad present.

My mother named me Ashley after her water boy in Haiti. Can you imagine a big black boy in Harlem with a name like Ashley? Needless to say, I hated the name and grew tired of being told it was a girl's name. When I entered corporate America, I legally changed my name to Ash, but I'm jumping ahead...

My Dad, Wesner Exantus, was born in Port-Au-Prince, Haiti, and was the 3rd of 8 children born from his mother (my grandmother). We're not sure where he falls in line with the additional nine children my grandfather had from different women, making my grandfather the father of a total of 17 children!

My dad never passed the 8th grade. His family was so poor that he needed to help out financially, so he enlisted in the Haitian Army when he was only 19 years old. You usually have to be 21, but one of his uncles worked at The Palais National (The National Palace), which was the official residence of the President of Haiti, and he pulled a favor to get him in early. Many of my dad's deployments were in different countries like West Germany and Israel. No longer aligned with his duties in the army, he decided to flee to France, then Canada, and eventually came to America at the age of 32 in 1974.

I'm not sure if he fell in love with my mom or if his marriage to her was an attempt to gain citizenship in the US, but they married in 1977, and he left in 1980 (when I was born) to go back to Haiti. In 1983, my dad returned with his two oldest daughters (Vivian and Kathleen). I'm not sure if my mom knew that my dad had other kids in Haiti, but she accepted them as her own with open arms, and we lived as a blended family. After a very tumultuous four years, my mom and dad divorced in 1987, and by 1988 we moved to the St. Nicholas Houses in Harlem, NY. This backdrop is very significant because this would shape my journey into manhood.

Now a single mom, she took a factory job making minimum wage to support the family and became ill due to long hours of standing on her feet. She stopped working in 1995 and started receiving disability benefits.

My mom grew up a devout believer in God. She started her spiritual journey in the Pentecostal church as a member of the Church of God of Manhattan. Once she moved to Harlem, she became a member of The Greater Refuge Temple, where she attended services every Tuesday and Sunday. Her dedication to God was evident in the way she greeted everyone by saying, "Praise the Lord" She even volunteered to hand out pamphlets in the streets to teach people about the love and power of God.

Mommy was selfless with a big heart. She was willing to give even with meager resources. Our home was open to anyone who needed it, and she never hesitated to feed the neighborhood. Everyone knew her as "Mommy" because she cared for others as her own children.

My mom loved me with her actions; however, in full transparency, I would verbally get berated often. I'm not sure if it was a "Haitian thing" or her version of tough love or a testament to the statement that "Hurt people, hurt people," but her words often pierced into my subconscious and created what I now realize was a sense of unworthiness.

Besides the "normal" tongue lashing of being "Salop, Kochon, Makak, Enbesil, Vakabon, Tet Kabrit, Bourick," which are all nice Haitian terms that mean Slob, Pig, Monkey, Imbecile, Hoodlum, Goat head, and Donkey, respectfully, I was also teased at home for being dark and for having a lazy eye (My mom was brown skin, and I was born with a condition called left ptosis where the muscle in my left eye are very weak, so my eyelid has a droop, the same condition that Forest Whitaker has).

My dad attempted to be in my life, but my mom would remind me that he wanted to abort me anytime he was around, so it was hard for me to ever open myself up to build a relationship with him. She would hit me with lines like… "Ou pa jwenn manman nan makèt," which translates to "You don't find mothers in the supermarket." She didn't mean this literally, but it was Beyoncé's Irreplaceable before Beyoncé. It was a reminder of all that she sacrificed for my siblings and me. Because of this, I shut down and became bitter, and held a dark disdain for my dad and most male authority figures.

My brother and I were eight years apart, and without a father figure in the household, my brother voluntarily tried to take on that role but not in a nurturing way. It was more of an authoritarian way where he punished me for acting up or not respecting him since I would never do what anybody said. This led to constant beatings from my mom and my brother. In the 90's beatings in the black community, especially if you were Caribbean, was normal. I'm talking about extension cord whippings, straight out the shower whippings, lay on your belly, and I'm gone beat your ass whippings— the type of stuff that would get a kid removed from the household today.

This turned me into a rebellious and angry young man wanting to take out my pain on everybody. I was always strong for my age, and even until this day; I have superhuman strength (which is why they call me Shaq on the basketball court).

I used my strength to fight as a kid, which resulted in my track record for getting suspended, kicked out and expelled from school. I got suspended more times than I can remember, kicked out in the 1st and 5th grade for fighting, in 9th grade for being too disruptive, then expelled in the 10th grade, not for fighting but for being at the wrong place at the wrong time. Because of my proximity to gang members, it was assumed I was gang-affiliated. Most of the young men in my neighborhood were Bloods, and a guy from my building (R.I.P.) was one of the founding members of the Nine-Trey Gangstas Blood set. While most of my friends became Bloods, I never joined a gang.

Growing up in the '90s was tough because most adults were either strung out on crack, alcoholics, or worked two or three jobs, so most preteens and teenagers had little to no supervision.

This meant that we would run around and do what we thought adults did without fearing any consequence. There was a lot of sexual activity happening at a very young age, among adults who had no business dealing with kids and with kids experimenting on each other.

My first-time having sex was at 11 years old with a young lady older than me and the aggressor. I didn't realize what was going on until she asked me what I was waiting for while laying in my bed with nothing on but a sundress. I'll spare you the details, but this sort of activity was normal. Either kids were having sex in apartments where parents weren't around, or the parents were around but too strung out on drugs to care. When we didn't have access to an apartment, we took our talents to the staircase, the big park, or the roof, aka Pebble Beach.

Luckily and unfortunately for us (And I mean this with all due respect), AIDS/HIV continued to be an epidemic and ran rampant in our community, so we saw people vanish before our eyes from the disease. So even though we were sexually free, most of us were careful and made sure we protected ourselves. Don't get me wrong, there were tons of chlamydia, gonorrhea, herpes, crabs, and syphilis stories, but for the most part, we did our best to stay safe.

Drinking and smoking at an early age was also a "normal" thing in my neighborhood. We were bombarded with Malt Liquor commercials telling us that we needed to drink a 40 ounce to be cool. So, drinking beer, smoking cigarettes, and playing spades were a pastime for us when we became teenagers. The first time I tried weed (Marijuana), I was 13 years old but hated the feeling of being high and not having control of my level of awareness and response time, so that was a habit that never formed. Besides, I developed a love for basketball and knew that if I wanted to get good at it, I needed to stay away from any drugs. At 12 years old, my friend Rodney (Rodbot) from elementary school was the first to convince me to try out for the school basketball team, and that's when I started taking it more seriously.

I was fortunate to have moved into the building that I moved into on 129th and 8th Avenue because it would give me front row access to crime at its highest level, so I never had to pretend that I wanted to live that life. My best friend Corey had an uncle who was a big deal in our neighborhood, so I was extended almost the same level of respect he had by mere association. Corey's sister hung out with my sister, and my mom was friendly with their grandmother. I spent a lot of time at his house, so his grandmother treated me like a grandson.

We would often eat at each other's houses, and I would see Corey's uncle and his friends in the hallway. They were part of a crew called Posse Deep, and they were highly respected. My association with Corey and his family did so much for me. First, it gave me the protection that I didn't know I needed, and secondly, it kept me from straying off the straight and narrow.

Other young kids dibbled and dabbled in the streets, but no one was having that when it came to Corey and me. They would beat me up if I wasn't in school, and they encouraged me to stick to playing basketball.

The men in Posse Deep were diverse. They all had me by at least ten years, so while I was 12 years old, they were in their early 20's. Some were gangsters with a capital G, and others went to work. Some were in the music business, and some were ladies' men. Some worked construction, and some worked the streets. Some were shooters on the court, and some were shooters who lived in court… criminal court, if you know what I mean. The diversity and access to them were important because they gave me a choice of who I wanted to emulate. Aqil Davidson from the legendary hip-hop group Wreckx-N-Effect was among those men.

I remember watching Aqil on TV doing his thing then see him in living color walking through the projects comfortably with a metal briefcase handcuffed to his wrist. (Well, maybe it wasn't handcuffed, but it was one of those briefcases that they usually handcuff to wrists in movies.) He and his crew threw free bus trips to amusement parks, fed the neighborhood on most holidays, and gave us a sense of pride to be from Harlem.

I didn't know how I would do it but seeing Aqil made me say that I want to be on TV and own a silver briefcase one day.

This proximity to young adults was also dangerous. I lived on the first floor, and my window faced the garbage disposal, so in addition to the unwanted rats and nasty smell, I was privy to seeing late-night beatings and pistol-whippings since that area was hidden and dark. It seemed like the perfect spot for criminal activity, and I heard and saw it all. I remember one night seeing a grown man fully naked being held up by four men while another man whipped him with a belt. The man was yelling for dear life. This experience scared me but didn't fully push me away from wanting to see more.

At the height of the crack era, there were so many shootouts daily, and since it became normal, every time we would hear them, we knew the routine, which was to get low and not get up until we heard it stop. Usually, when the gunfire ceased, my friends and I would run towards the gunsmoke to see if anyone got hit. We were usually lucky not to run into anyone, but one day we heard the gunshots and ran towards the gunsmoke, and there laid a man who met his untimely demise. My friends and I stood over the body, shocked in disbelief, while elders were screaming at us from the adjacent windows telling us to get away from the body. We were so shocked that we didn't hear them, and it took one of the OG's from the neighborhood to snatch us up and take us away. Unfortunately, this wouldn't be the last time I saw someone shot, but these experiences taught me a few things about life. 1) You never know when your time is up, and 2) If you play by street rules, you are liable to suffer street consequences.

Because of this, I never really had a desire to be someone who lived the street life. Don't get me wrong I had my share of mischief, and my friends and I constantly had to fight other crews to gain our respect, but I was mainly an entrepreneur at heart. My mom barely spoke English and could only make meager ends working at a factory to support herself and three children. Even though I was the youngest, instinctively, I knew that I needed to do something to help make ends meet. Similar to the decision that my parents made back in Haiti.

Every time we would go to the supermarket, I noticed young people bagging up the groceries and getting money in return (this was when young kids held those positions). So instead of hanging out in the park, I started hanging out around the supermarket, trying to figure out how I could be one of those kids who got the opportunity to pack bags.

One day luck would have it that the regular bag packers didn't show up,

and the cashiers at the supermarket needed someone to fill in. Because I was around so much, I got my opportunity. In my mind, I wanted this opportunity to last more than one day, so instead of just filling in, I went above and beyond to make sure that everyone would feel my presence in a good way.

I worked from the time the supermarket opened until they closed, and because I lived on the first floor, I would run across the street, bang on the window, and just throw money at my mom and then run back to grab my spot. Being able to give my mom money was a great feeling because it made me feel like I was the man of the house.

This experience at eight years old taught me the importance of customer service, so I smiled at every customer, made small talk with the cashiers, and even helped stock boxes during downtime. After that day, I was given priority over some of the usual bag packers and eventually became a regular myself. My new status didn't necessarily go well with those that were there before me, so on occasion, there were little scuffles and scraps over spots, but for the most part, I had a solid four-year run at the Bravo Supermarket.

By 12 years old, I graduated from packing bags at the supermarket to selling T-shirts and mixtapes on 125th St. I never knew this was even an option until one day I took a break and saw Stephen, one of my neighborhood friends, walking by with a bunch of T-shirts, harassing people to buy them. I ran to him and said, "yo, where you get those shirts from?" He replied, "I work for Kool-Aid now!" Kool-Aid was a famous street vendor on 125th St. and had an army of young kids working for him.

What was great about working for a vendor was that the kids were selling the shirts for $20, keeping $5 from every sale, and giving the vendor back $15. This was a win-win for everybody because all the vendor had to do was manage the inventory. The kids would sell shirts easier because the crime was so rampant that the people who came to shop at 125th St. were happy to see productive children. In essence, we were selling our charm and productivity more than we were selling the products.

Doing the math in my head, if I spent all day at the supermarket packing bags, I made between $15 and $35. As a street vendor, I could sell four shirts in an hour and make what I was making on most days in the store. Now, if I worked the whole day as I did at the supermarket, I would make ten times the amount I made packing bags. Once I realized that, I knew that I too needed to work for Kool-Aid.

Kool-Aid had his operation like a well-oiled machine, and I guess word got out about his arrangement with the youth because you would see kids from all over Harlem crowding his van trying to get work.

What I didn't know was that you couldn't just ask to work for him if he didn't know you or if you weren't referred to him by someone he knew. It was a trust factor there because he's giving you his shirts on consignment and has to trust that you will return with his money. I kept trying to get his attention and get him to give me shirts without a co-sign, but I was denied left and right.

Regardless of being denied, I still knew this was what I needed to be doing, so I would just show up and hope that he would give me a shot. Right next to him was another vendor named Rich Kid. Rich Kid had a great personality, everyone knew him, he also gave out opportunities to the youth. One Saturday, I came by again to try to get on Kool-Aid's team, and Rich Kid called me over to him (maybe because he kept seeing me all the time) and said, "Yo whatsup Shorty! What you trying to do?" I said, "I'm trying to be down on Kool-Aid's team!" After a series of questions, he started me out with a few shirts and told me to sell them.

At first, I didn't leave 125th St. and set up a table to get sales, after a while Rich Kid began to trust me and I could go to him and get merchandise to sell freely. I began to roam around Harlem and sell shirts and mixtapes in the streets, salons, barbershops, and even the number spots. Like clockwork, I would come back and give Rich Kid his money, and all was well. Street vending lasted for a few years until I was old enough to work summer youth and decided to do that instead. Ironically a program implemented to help the youth made us lazy because with the Summer Youth Employment Program you didn't have to work hard, and you would still get paid. Being an employee was different from packing bags or being a vendor because you eat what you kill (meaning if you don't work, you don't eat). The introduction of Government and City jobs took away ambition from many young people, disincentivized hard work, and introduced paycheck paralysis to the youth.

As my friends and I got older, some of us stayed on the straight and narrow, and others decided to dip our toes in the street life. Regardless of which side we chose most of us still got our hands dirty. See in the hood (Similar to how it is in jail) even if you didn't want to fight, if you were tested then you had to defend yourself quick and fast because if you didn't, you became a target and as Jay-Z said in The Streets is Watching, "Once you're tagged lame, the game is follow the leader." We had a lot of loyalty in our hood so we would fight against other crews in our same projects but if anyone ever came from other blocks to test us, then God bless their souls. St. Nicholas Projects had a notorious reputation for wanting all the smoke, so no one played with us that much. On occasion when outsiders would test us, our crews formed like Voltron to hold our neighborhood down. One of the leaders of the pack was Dedric but went by the name Bad News; he was a skilled boxer, so his hand game was immaculate, and he was also being groomed by the other gangsters in the neighborhood, so his gun game was on point as well. Growing up he was our protector; if we ever got into any beef externally, he was the one who made sure we can go to other blocks to fight and leave out alive. If it ever escalated to anything above fighting, we didn't have to worry about it because he and his crew MNM (Money N Murder) would hold us down.

I continued to hustle on the street selling merch and fixing bikes for a fee and got serious about playing basketball. I got so good at basketball that I was in at least 2-3 basketball tournaments at a time. I tried out for the elite AAU teams like Riverside and Gauchos but never seemed to get picked since I wasn't extra tall or super-fast. I was strong and had a quick baseline game, but that wasn't enough. I had a house full of trophies, so I was always on the winning teams and contributed tremendously to every team. I was fortunate to play for the Milbank Flyers and Little East, where I gained the nickname "Mr Baseline" by AL Cash, legendary commentator from Rucker Park. I also won a few chips (championships) at my home court tournament Byrd Classics. I played in NYCHA leagues, PAL, and citywide, so my days were busy. Basketball saved my life. I learned a lot of valuable lessons about life and team building from playing ball. The friends who decided to dip their toes in the streets were constantly going to jail. Whether it was the Spofford Juvenile Detention Center in the Bronx or Rikers Island's Infamous C74, I got accustomed to hearing horror stories and war tales about jail life. On occasion, I would go with my friend's parents (mother in most cases) to visit my friends to keep them abreast of what was going on in the streets and motivate them to keep their heads up. This was happening when I was between 15 and 16 so, balancing entrepreneurship, basketball, jail visits, and keeping up with the ladies was exhausting.

This was also around the time that the infamous and unfair 94 crime bill was introduced so all of our OG's were getting locked up at record numbers leaving a whole generation to figure things out for themselves. I don't glorify crime at all but before the crime bill, the streets were organized. There was respect for the Gangsters who came before so the current gangsters had wise counsel to lean on.

There was also an obvious divide and respect for elders, women, children, and civilians; meaning that if you weren't part of the street life you didn't have to worry about getting caught in the crossfire. The 94' crime bill disproportionately dismantled our neighborhood because it imposed mandatory life sentences for individuals with three or more felony convictions and levied harsh new penalties for justice-involved youth which exacerbated the school-to-prison pipeline specifically for black children. Because of these mandatory minimums and how focused politicians were on seeming tough on crime to "super predators" they also enforced the RICO Law which was passed in 1970. RICO stands for the Racketeer Influenced and Corrupt Organizations Act and is a federal law designed to combat organized crime in the United States. It allowed prosecution and civil penalties for racketeering activity performed as part of an ongoing criminal enterprise and was mainly used for those who were part of the Mob. Now because it was being used to lock up black and brown bodies; people who weren't even involved in the streets were getting targeted and locked up and law enforcement didn't have to prove that they were involved in a crime, all they had to do was draw a connection (even if it was hearsay).

Once the streets were wiped clean, my generation and below created new street rules and that's when the chaos began.

At this time, two of my childhood friends decided that they would jump all the way into the hustlers' lifestyle by becoming drug dealers and started their own operation. Most of the drug dealers we knew were older but because there was an opening my friends decided to fill that void. Seeing them take on that role at such a young age was something we didn't see in our projects. Sure, we heard the stories about Rich Porter, AZ, and Alpo getting money at a young age, but by the time I came up, the young guys weren't the ones with the packs; they were probably working for someone else who was significantly older.

In the beginning, they weren't making that much money, but eventually, they started to kill it. I think I was maybe a year older than them, so at 16, these guys were making so much money that they started buying jewelry, dressing up in designer clothes, and even had expensive cars. One of the two was a real ladies' man, so not only did his money enhance his ability to attract the hottest girls in town but being able to drive around with him in his different whips enhanced those benefits for those who were close to him too.

At this point, I'm looking at the "little money" I'm making selling mixtapes here and there and then looking at what my friends are making, and my first thought was maybe I should get money with them!

In my household, my sister and I built a strong bond. We would run everything by each other and support each other no matter what. She was working at a video store called Blockbuster Videos and had just been promoted to assistant manager. Because she had this job, every time new sneakers would come out; I would negotiate with her to give me money to buy Jordans or clothes. The roles had reversed because even though she was older, I would always lend her money when she needed it. I was used to having my own money, so it felt weird being at the mercy of someone else and I wasn't making money fast enough.

When the opportunity to sell drugs with my friends came up, I ran it by my sister to see what she thought. Immediately she started yelling at me, getting up in my face and we ended up almost having a fistfight because she was so angry that I would even jeopardize my freedom for some clothes and sneakers. What she was most angry about was what my mother would think if she ever found out I was selling drugs or worse if I got arrested or killed because I decided to be part of the street life.

I was hard-headed and had decided to sell drugs, so I put the wheels in motion to get my first pack. I was tired of knock-off branded clothes or sewing patches on jeans to look like I had money. My sister, also hardheaded, wouldn't let it go, and eventually, she got me so frustrated that I said, "All right! If you don't want me to sell drugs, then get me a job! If you get me a job, then I won't sell drugs!" That's all she needed to hear. At the time, I didn't mean it; I just thought that she would leave me alone if I said that to her. In true big sister fashion, she told one of her manager friends from another store what was going on and I believe that on the strength of her reputation, he wanted to help her save her baby brother, so he gave me a job.

At 17, I was working at the video store instead of selling drugs, and every day after school I would go to the Blockbuster on 17th Street and Eighth Avenue and work as a video clerk. I am naturally competitive, so anything I see someone doing, I'm always thinking about how I can match the effort or do it better. Many young people were assistant managers across the Blockbuster video network, so I immediately set my sights on that. I was always willing to put in work, and anytime someone needed a helping hand, I would work at my store and other stores. Within a year, I built a reputation as someone who is hard-working and received a promotion to assistant manager within a year. By this time, I was transferred to the video store on 8th and Broadway, where I worked with Edwin Cintron and assistant managers LaShawn Miles and Tangie Webb. Remember these names because they're sure to pop up again.

We were a strong unit, really like family, and because Edwin always had us striving to be the best, we would often come in on our days off to help out. We were always there to pitch in if the store got busy or somebody needed a replacement because they were dealing with something outside of work. We always did our best to be the #1 store in our district, which meant us keeping our loss prevention numbers down. Since we were downtown and the stores were always crowded, boosters would always come to the store and try to steal everything you could think of: movies, DVDs, candy, soda, toys;

you name it, if we sold it, they tried to steal it. Being young and still from the hood, I defended the store like I was defending my block. I would run and chase people trying to steal and had a few scuffles with people who didn't want to back down. We also started selling memberships, and because of my entrepreneurship skills, I was the top seller in the store. To pay forward the opportunity that my sister gave me, I also was able to get a few friends jobs to help them get off the streets. For some, the money wasn't coming fast enough, and they didn't last long. A lot of them also didn't see the benefit of working retail in the long term. They lost the forest for the tree, not realizing that their skills in retail would help them in a career later.

On the other hand, I knew that Blockbuster wouldn't be my last stop. By my 19th birthday, Edwin was approached by an old colleague to work as a manager at Citibank. This was an excellent opportunity to go from blockbuster videos to a world-renowned bank. Naturally, he jumped on the opportunity and left our team at Blockbuster. His replacement was a young guy who was probably not too much older than me but worked in the system longer than I did, and he was close with the district manager at the time. Even though I didn't want the position, it felt weird reporting to somebody close to my age, especially as a teenager because he had to be no older than 21, and he was from Brooklyn. To give that statement context, I went to Martin Luther King HS and in King-- Brooklyn and Harlem didn't get along. We thought they were grimey and we never really trusted them.

My sister Tangie was from Brooklyn, but she was an exception. LaShawn and I were Harlemites, so we adopted her as one of our own. The three of us kept our bond, but it wasn't the same without Edwin there. Because this new store manager was young, he had something to prove, and he didn't come in there trying to be our friend. He had an agenda and was making sure that we knew he was the boss. Usually, when a new manager takes over a store, they would fire most staff and bring in their people to make it successful.

Because we were already successful, it was hard to just fire us, so he didn't make coming to work fun.

LaShawn didn't play that and wasn't going to wait like a sitting duck so she was trying to find her way out of Blockbuster as soon as she could, so in addition to working at our store, she got a job at Chase Bank as a teller. She was working both jobs for a few months and one day came into the store and told us that Chase had an open house for Tellers. I knew that since the environment at the store had changed, it was time for me to make my exit, and I jumped at the opportunity. At 19 years old, I got my first job as a teller, and that's where the fun started. I attempted to work at Chase in the morning and Blockbuster on the nights and weekends, but this was exhausting and wasn't worth it, so I quit Blockbuster shortly after.

After three weeks of teller training down at the main Chase site at the World Trade Center, I got placed at the two Penn Plaza Chase branch right across the street from Madison Square Garden. This was considered a mega branch because we had two floors, a branch manager, sales manager, service manager, two teller managers, financial advisors, business bankers, private bankers, consumer bankers, and over 15 tellers. This branch also had high foot traffic because of our location so there wasn't too much downtime. Because I had experience as an assistant manager at Blockbuster videos and learned how to be a good leader, working as a teller came easy. It is my philosophy that in order for one to become a great leader one must know how to become a great follower. Knowing how to put myself in my manager's shoes helped me go above and beyond and ultimately shine in every position I ever held.

We had two teller managers, one was a middle-aged black woman and the other was a young man of Filipino descent. Seeing this young man inspired me because I looked at working at the bank as a prestigious job, so seeing him rise to manager made me believe that I could do the same. Our first branch manager was a white woman named Eileen and she was nice but really went by the book.

Within my third month at the bank, she was being transferred out to a bigger branch and being replaced by a young black man named Michael Black. His family was from Jamaica so he spoke with a slight Jamaican/British accent, but he was very sharp; his suits were always expensive, and you could tell that he was the manager by the way he talked and walked. Immediately, I set my sights on that role. Representation matters, so seeing someone young managing such an important branch made me want to do that as well. I knew from my days at Blockbuster what it took to get promoted... You simply have to go above and beyond in your current position so that the powers that be can envision you doing something else and being more valuable in the position you want. In essence, you have to outgrow your current position.

The male tellers didn't have to wear a suit, we only had to wear slacks, a shirt, and tie but for those who were bankers or customer service representatives, a suit was required. Having that knowledge, I decided to start wearing suits. In the beginning, some of the tellers would joke about me because they thought I was kissing up or trying to get on the good side of my manager... They were right! I was doing all that and I really didn't care what the tellers thought about me. I had a different mindset and regardless of the level of work; whether it's retail, office work, or a profession, the rules are the same and I've been here before.

I knew that if I "looked the part" when an opportunity arose, I would be ready instead of scrambling to get ready. After two months of wearing a suit behind the teller line and providing customers with the best service I can provide them, my opportunity came when one of the customer service reps had to leave to go on maternity leave. She would be out for three months and because of the way personnel are distributed at the bank, a three-month leave didn't automatically allow our branch to get someone to replace her for such a small amount of time. This meant that customer service reps had to deal with the shortage for 90 days. Since we were a commuter branch right at Penn Plaza and Madison Square Garden, during lunchtime it often got really busy and the customer service reps would get frustrated all the time with lines backing up. As a man on a mission to get to the next level, I would throw on my suit jacket and voluntarily ask people on the line what they needed help with. If it was something simple, I would tell them to go to my teller window and I would take care of the transaction for them or look up what they needed. Eventually, some of the customers were so used to me knowing how to manage their simple requests that they wouldn't even stop at customer service, they would just come to me directly. This meant that the service line was shorter, and the branch got fewer complaints about long waits. This caught the attention of the service manager, Anne who would now ask me to cover for some of the customer service reps while they were out to lunch.

In the beginning, I wasn't logging onto any system, I was simply directing traffic but one of the customer service reps, Jackie Marriott noticed me taking initiative and saw how ambitious I was, so she decided to take me under her wing and allow me to use her system to take care of basic transactions. My brother is a computer genius and has been building them since before they were in everyone's household, so he taught me a thing or two about computer software. Those lessons came in handy at the bank because the system they used was MS-DOS which was the operating system that provided the most security for bank transactions at the time. This was the year 2000 so we just got through the Y2K scare and the systems we were using were new for everyone. I eventually learned the system so well that even though I was still a teller they gave me access to the customer service system and I became an unofficial member of the customer service team.

The other tellers were big mad! They would joke about how officially my title was teller, but I was being used to sign on to do customer service work. Any time the teller line was short, and they needed me to help out, the other tellers would give me this look like "ha ha you're back here with us." It was all good because I had a bigger plan in mind, and I knew that this was just a steppingstone to what I really wanted. After three months of being on the customer service team, the rep that was out on maternity leave came back and all my hatin-ass teller coworkers were looking forward to me joining them back at the teller line. To be fair it wasn't all of them. I had a few allies who rooted for me, but the majority prayed for my downfall.

Being sent back to the teller line is exactly what happened, and it was discouraging at first, but the experience was something that they couldn't take away from me. I was "promoted" to the business teller window which gave me more responsibility, but it wasn't where I wanted to be. Regardless of that I continued to do my job with excellence and worked as a business teller for two months. As energetic alignment would have it, one of the personal bankers was getting transferred to another location and instead of looking for a replacement from another branch, the sales manager loved what I did as a fill-in for customer service, so she allowed me to interview for the role. In less than a year of working at the bank, I was officially promoted to a personal banker, one month before my 20th birthday.

For the next few years, I would prove to be one of the top personal bankers not only in my branch but in the whole tri-state area. I used my entrepreneurial skills and charm to reach all of my sales quotas and then some. The advantages I had over the other bankers were that I was a teller, so I knew what their goals were and how to incentivize them to send me clients... even the ones hating on me initially. The bankers didn't realize that the tellers saw 80% of the customers and only 20% would ever stop at the customer service counter to see a banker. So, while the bankers are in their fancy suits, sitting behind their desk, dialing for dollars, a person they just left a message for was at the teller window laughing with the very teller they refuse to acknowledge. After becoming a banker, I realized why tellers hated the bankers or anyone trying not to be a teller anymore. It was because everyone treated the tellers like they were the lowest on the totem pole, but the truth was without tellers the bank couldn't even function. Yes, it was an entry-level position, but they were the ones that had the real relationships with the customers so the right co-sign from them could help you reach all of your goals.

Because I knew what type of clients I was looking for, I spent time in the back training the tellers on reaching their referral numbers and giving them tips and clues on what type of clients would make good referrals. This ultimately put money in their pockets, so they loved me and sent me everyone. By the time the other bankers realized what I was doing, it was too late because I had already gained the trust of most of the tellers.

I was officially the man! I was winning awards, getting recognition, and building a solid clientele of clients who not only did business with me but referred their friends to me as well.

I was also still a lady's man and since I was tall, handsome and successful, being able to attract the girls was something that came easy. One of my teller friends Jason and I would always flirt with either the pretty tellers or the pretty customers that came into our branch. We would bet each other who could get girls' numbers first, and it became a thing where we would compete against each other to see who could sleep with the most girls.

I was also attending college at the same time, so not only was I busy working, I was also learning full-time at night at the Borough of Manhattan Community College (BMCC), working on my associate's degree in finance and investments. Between work and school, I didn't have time for a real relationship so juggling multiple girls to meet my needs was my norm. I was careful so I didn't have a reputation for sleeping around which worked in my favor when it came to having multiple steady "friends." I had a friend at school, a friend at work, and a friend from the neighborhood. I also had casual friends who were always phone calls away or those who I met at a party or club. To say without saying, life was good and there was infinite abundance in the romance area. This was so much the case that I barely had to ask girls for what I needed; they already knew. I had this undefeated record where once a girl came to my house the get down always went down.

With full transparency, I used my relationship with girls for one thing and one thing only. I never really respected their minds or intellect, but this changed when I met this young lady at my job who was everything, I never knew I needed. She was gorgeous with a banging body, smart, confident, and had a little bit of hood in her. I remember when I first saw her at the Bank's Christmas party with one of the tellers from my branch. I immediately tried to introduce myself, but I think the teller she was with liked me, so she wasn't trying to make any real introductions. A few months later the young lady was transferred to my branch, and this is where the games begin.

I remember the first time I saw her sitting at the teller window, I immediately ran to my friend Jason like, "Yo! Who that!" He was like "Don't even waste your time cause she won't even talk to you, I tried." He said this as if because he tried to talk to her and failed that I had no shot. As a competitive being I laughed and said, "Watch me work!" He was confident that I couldn't get her, and I was confident that I could so he bet me $20 that I couldn't get her number, I took it a step further and said I bet I can sleep with her. I immediately went to work by observing her and plotting on how to get her attention.

At this point, I'm 21 years old, very charming, and personable with the tellers because as you remember I used them as a referral source for client prospects. As I made my usual rounds, I noticed two things, she was a reader, so she always had a book close to her and she kept to herself except for her one friend Mavis that she always went to lunch with. I wasn't a reader by any stretch of the imagination and by this time I could only remember reading two books in my life, A message to the Black Man by Elijah Muhammad when I was 13 and Of mice to men when I was 15, other than that the closest I came to reading was Don Diva, FEDs, The Vibe and Source magazine.

One day I noticed her reading this thick book that was maybe about 700 pages long (no exaggeration), called Before the Mayflower. I pretended to be interested in the book and introduced myself by asking her what she was reading. She told me what it was about, then I bought it the following week. I would skim through it and pick up random places in the book to read and go talk to her about. She was very intrigued, and this led to us conversing a few times while we were at work. I had the gift of gab, so I could hold a conversation as if I read the book all the while I hadn't really picked it up.

If this deception weren't enough, I also would time when she went to lunch to "accidentally" bump into her as if I was going to lunch at the same time. See, the tellers had scheduled lunchtimes, so if I snuck in the back and looked at the schedule, I would know who went when. Because I was a personal banker, as long as other bankers were on the banking floor to manage the incoming customers, I could take lunch anytime I wanted. This accidental bumping into each other happened often but it was usually three of us since she would go to lunch with her friend Mavis. One day I believe Mavis was out and my crush was going to lunch by herself and so as she picked up her stuff to leave, I ran downstairs to re-create another "accidental" meeting. As I'm coming up the escalator she's going down and I asked her where she was going, and she said lunch, so I ran back downstairs and accompanied her. This first encounter led to other encounters and eventually we went out on a date.

I remember like it was yesterday. It was Friday, March 22, 2002; we went to Times Square to watch Blade II by Wesley Snipes. Our lips were locked for most of the movie, so I don't really remember if the movie was good or not. I was still in school at BMCC and took Saturday classes. Energetic alignment would have it that the following day after our date, I had class and as I'm walking down the hall, I see a long line of people waiting for something. I wasn't really looking at anyone's face, but something pulled me towards this couple. As I walked by them, it was her; SMH! She was with another guy who was obviously her boyfriend because he was either holding her or standing so close that it couldn't be anything else. My street instincts kicked in, and I just played it cool and said hi and kept it pushing. She responded, and the boyfriend had this confused look on his face like "How do you know him" I peeked over to see their interaction and it was as if she told him in a nonchalant way that we worked together and left it at that.

The following Monday, when I saw her at work, she told me that the line was for a job interview as a School Safety Officer for which she had to take a test. She also came clean that what I suspected was true that the gentleman was indeed her boyfriend. I never really cared if a girl had a boyfriend or not but for some reason, I wanted to respect her and her relationship. In fact, I found that with my busy schedule it was best to deal with girls that had boyfriends because I wouldn't be obligated to the responsibility of being a boyfriend while reaping the benefits (or sharing the benefits.)

Maybe it was the way she carried herself, but I didn't look at her as just someone I wanted to sleep with; I wanted to get to know her. I stopped pursuing her so hard and just kept our relationship casual. I would still go to lunch with her and Mavis occasionally, but it wasn't as calculated as before. She ended up quitting the bank abruptly, and the only time I would speak to her was on the phone. As we stayed in contact, she told me that she had broken up with her boyfriend, so I was ready to shoot my shot again.

One day, my friend Greg had extra tickets to "Russel Simmon's: Def Poetry Jam" and asked me if I wanted to go. He was bringing a date, so I called my crush to go with me and she agreed. Greg and I met when I was 12 years old when we played basketball together on the same team. He was from 134th street but hung out on my block (129th). We hung out with different crews but still managed to stay cool. During my senior year in High School Greg and I grew closer because one of his friends Carlos went to my school and Carlos and I hung out every day. In fact, Carlos's dad sold me my first car when I was 18; a sky blue 1988 Pontiac Bonneville that we affectionately called Bonnie. Greg would eventually become my right-hand man. My family became his family and vice versa. In fact, I called his mom, Mama and his dad, Pops. Greg was known as a popular battle rapper in Harlem that went by the name of G-Child. He was a smart guy and went to a top high school for Basketball but was also a little bit crazy. He was one of those guys that if he felt disrespected, he would black out and put hands on whoever he felt disrespected him. He also didn't really have any filter, so he was known to piss people off with his words both friends and foes.

The Def Poetry Jam show was great, and everything was going well but my date, (whose name is Amina by the way) kept going to the bathroom on more than one occasion. After the show was over, I saw her talking on her cell phone and the energy just felt weird. We were planning to get something to eat after the show, but once we left the venue, it was almost like déjà vu… just like before, this strange guy was staring at her and asking her questions. Come to find out it was the same boyfriend as before but based on her account they were no longer together. Apparently, she was telling him it's over, but he wasn't ready to let that happen just yet. She told him she was on a date not thinking he would be crazy enough to interfere, but he pulled up on us.

Greg and I were both big guys… Both over 6 feet and over 200 lbs. We're both also pretty nice with our hands and pride ourselves with having a "One hitter quitter" which means that if we hit you by surprise, you're probably not gonna get up. I could tell by looking in this guy's eyes that he wasn't built the way we were built so nothing in me told me to take it to a level that it didn't need to go. We were also in Times Square so if any commotion happened, the cops would've gotten to us within a New York minute. In the beginning, her boyfriend was calm but as she started to ask him what he was doing there, he started getting louder and louder.

At this point, I was concerned for her because I didn't know if he would try to put his hands on her or not, so I stepped in to make sure everything was OK. He immediately looked at me and said "I knew there was something. It's you from her job." I laughed because now I realize it was the same guy that was with her at BMCC. I looked at him and told him to calm down; I said "Fam, it's all good, you don't want this to go someplace else." He looked at me and said, "Fam, it's all good, you don't want this to go someplace else." I said, "all right now I'm trying to tell you" He said, "all right now I'm trying to tell you." I then realized he was saying everything that I was saying so I thought to myself that this guy isn't all there.

Greg finally gets wind of what's going on and comes charging over to us like a madman. (I told you he was a little crazy.) I literally had to restrain him from trying to put hands on this guy because Greg stayed on ready. On top of that, Greg called one of our OG's who was really with the shits, and he was on his way to us, to make sure everything was ok, so this was about to get ugly really fast. Our OG rarely talked so whenever there were real problems he's the guy you called. This wasn't that so I did my best to call off all that was about to go down.

After this encounter, I officially said that I was going to stop communicating with her. My life was practically drama-free, so this was too much to add to my plate, especially because I was still on a professional mission.

I continued to excel at work and at school and by the time I was 23 I was one of the top bankers in the tri-state based on fixed annuity sales, home equity and mortgage sales, and all of my tellers were top referrers. I also was able to make the Dean's list 4 times at BMCC. Because I started my banking career as a teller, the amount of money I was making didn't reflect my all-star status. My managers would give me small incremental increases every time it was time for a raise, but I was making pennies compared to my older counterparts who weren't bringing in half of the business that I was. This was far from fair because the older bankers or people who came in with no experience got paid almost double what I was being paid.

I knew my worth and expressed my concern to my bosses, but they stated there was nothing they could do since policies and procedures capped the amount of money someone can receive as a raise all at one time. I was fed up that a mere technicality meant that I would have to suffer for my greatness. I reached out to my old boss Edwin from Blockbuster because he was now working at Citibank, and I told him my dilemma. As I was telling him the numbers, I was pulling in he wasn't surprised because he knew my abilities based of our past experience working together. He said, "Let me set you up with an appointment with one of the branches uptown. I know they have an opening and I think you'll be a great fit." I interviewed at Citibank on 96th and Broadway and was offered the job almost on the spot and they agreed to pay me twice as much money as I was making at Chase. With an offer letter in hand, I went to the bank to resign. Like a governmental pardon, my sales manager and branch manager made a call to the regional office to get me a raise and an officer title. By 24, I was a VP at one of the largest global banks in the country and making more than people who are twice my age. This felt great, and I was high off life.

At this point, I was still dating multiple girls, but it was distracting because greater success was what I had on my mind. I kept thinking about Amina and out of the blue I decided to give her a call. I remember this like clockwork, I called her cell phone and got her voicemail and left a message for her to call me back. As I waited by the phone, the branch started to get busy, so I asked my coworker

Erica if my phone rang, please pick it up and only come get me if it was Amina. So, I'm in the back with the tellers and Erica comes running to the back telling me that Amina was on the phone. I dropped everything I was doing, and we reconnected.

I won't belabor this love story but apparently, she was able to shake free of her crazy boyfriend, so we started to date exclusively. The timing was impeccable because even though I was successful as a banker I still had an allure of the street life. I was making so much money, but all of my money went to buying clothes. I was still living with my mom in the projects and her rent was less than $500 per month so when I pitched in it didn't make a dent in my pockets.

I was officially hood rich, and when I wasn't wearing a suit, I dressed like how the guys who were getting money dressed, and I was getting the same attention they were getting. In fact, I loved the attention so much that every time I got off of work, I would run to my building's back entrance, hoping no one saw me so I could change and get into my fresh street gear. I never claimed to be a street hustler, but I didn't want anyone to know that I had a 9-5 either.

Because my income status changed, I started hanging out with some of the top hustlers in Harlem. That life was different. I was making good money as a 24-year-old, but the type of money they saw was different. I didn't know what type of business they were in, but they were the first serial entrepreneurs I've seen. They had barbershops, clothing stores, restaurants, nice cars, houses, and of course, women. My childhood best friend Quise is the one who introduced me to this life. Quise and I have been friends since I was eight years old, and he has been by my side through every up and down I've ever had in my life. Around this time, Quise was testing his foot in the Gangster life waters. He had been mentored by one of our OG's and was making a transition into that life. Think of Mike's transition if you ever saw season 4 of the award-winning drama series, The Wire (Tristan Wilds' character). Our OG, Quise, Bad

News (Who had just come home from doing an 8-year bid), and my other OG M3 had formed an alliance and started hanging out on 8th Avenue. Since Quise and Bad News were my guys, I would hang with them after work, and eventually, I became part of the fold. 8th Avenue was a hot spot, and the respect these four guys had in Harlem meant that everybody who was anybody would stop to show love.

One of the guys I met during this time was my now Big Bro Jab. No one ever knew what Jab was into, but he stayed fresh, had money, and was always connected with business deals outside of the hood norm. Jab walked in his greatness but was humble, so I was attracted to his way of life. I remember one day, Jab taking me to a meeting with some of his other homies at an expensive restaurant downtown. This was the first time I've ever been to that type of restaurant where the food was so expensive that they didn't even put the price on the menu. I knew I had it but I still wanted to know what things cost so every time I ordered, I would ask Jab "how much is this? how much is that?" and he would look at me with this face like "Bro, be easy! just order what you want." Once the bill came, I was ready to pull out my debit card and pay for my portion, and just like real hustlers, they were arguing over who would pay the whole bill. This experience opened my eyes to how abundance and financial freedom truly felt. M3 would also take me around to different spots and neighborhoods so between Jab and M3 I was exposed to so many top-level money makers.

Everywhere we went the red carpet was rolled out. I remember going to a spot and didn't have to wait in line at all, in fact, we weren't even searched; we just went in as if we owned every spot. This attention attracted two types of people: those who loved you and wanted to be part of that experience and those who were haters and wanted to stop your flow.

Now I'm living a double life, one during the day as a bank officer and then at night hanging with the Harlem hustlers. This was also the beginning of banking crossing over into the hood where tellers were being coerced into giving bank information up to those who wanted to defraud customers. I knew this type of fraud firsthand because I worked as a banker and for most of the customers that had someone steal their identity, I was the one filing the fraud claims for them.

Because of my connection to the bank and my connections to the streets, I was often approached about supplying bank account information and account numbers. To be 100% transparent, the amount of money they were offering me was very tempting, but the truth is that I worked so hard to get to the position that I was in that no amount of money was worth my career or reputation. Plus, I got to know most of my clients personally so there was no way I would betray that trust.

Besides the mounting pressure of my street friends trying to get me to become a supplier of customers' bank information to commit fraud, there was also a civil war brewing in my neighborhood. Old friends became enemies, and they were looking to harm each other. More specifically, the young Gs were trying to make a name for themselves vs. the Older Gs that had already put in the work and violence ensued immediately after. Shootings and senseless killings became the norm during this period and the streets became a more dangerous place for those who were involved including innocent bystanders.

There was also news that the cops were looking to crack down on illegal activity and started rounding up the usual suspects in the neighborhood because of the shootings. One day, one of the usual suspects was picked up and glanced at the pictures of the remaining pickups that the cops planned to make and he noticed that a picture of me was part of the pile.

Between the shootings and being on the usual suspects' list, I started to feel as if these were signs that I needed to distance myself from the street life. Imagine getting caught up in street beef, potentially being shot, killed, or arrested while being a VP at a major bank; that just didn't make any sense.

At this point, I started taking my work and relationship with Amina seriously. When I wasn't at work, I would be with her and slowly but surely, she became my first official girlfriend. She also officially broke my undefeated "if I take you home, I'm sleeping with you" record because she made me wait 2 years before we slept together. She held herself with so much respect which is probably why I fell in love with her so fast. She also challenged me intellectually, more than anyone has ever challenged me. I was already a powerhouse, but she was making me better.

Even though things were going well at the bank, I still had an itch for continuing my journey as an entrepreneur. It was in my blood, and it was something that I did since eight years old so when Greg came to me with this idea about starting a record label, I immediately jumped at it.

See, Greg got signed to a label deal with Alicia Keys when he was only 21 straight after graduating college. The label deal did not work out because of creative differences, but everyone in the neighborhood saw his potential as a rap star. His idea was to join forces with another dope rapper in Harlem named Kev Starks, the best DJ in Harlem, DJ GetOnUp, and Kimbo (A young entrepreneur and investor)- together, we were StreetHeat Entertainment. Because of my background in banking, I managed the business and kept the books together. The idea behind StreetHeat was to create a movement that would highlight other dope rappers in our town while helping to shine a light on Greg and Kev Starks.

We planned to start in Harlem but then eventually move out to different cities throughout the US. Our first project was a mixtape called Hell Up in Harlem and featured some then up and coming but now internationally known rappers like Munda Mook, T-Rex, Jae Millz, Cardan, Skotch Davis, Charlie Clips, Smoke Dza, amongst others.

By this time, I learned that if you want anything to be successful, you have to go all-in, so to commit to this project fully, I decided to quit my job at the bank. Quitting my job came as a shock to everyone because I was doing so well and making so much money. Even though the money would've helped our venture, I knew that I needed to be active in this venture, so working 60-70 hours a week at the bank then giving the rest of my time to StreetHeat wouldn't cut it.

Because I believed in my ability as a salesperson, I decided to supplement my income and help fund our new endeavor; I would work as an independent contractor for Aflac. I kept seeing the commercials on TV, and the concept seemed pretty straightforward. The rationale was that if I am a full-time employee, my job controls my time, but if I was an independent contractor, I could do what I feel.

Greg had also decided to quit his job to commit to making StreetHeat a success, and he joined me in selling Aflac. We had some moderate success, but we realized immediately that starting a business as an independent contractor wasn't as easy as it sounds. It takes a lot of focus and dedication to be successful; it wasn't something you could do on the side. Especially when you get paid on commission, which means you "eat what you kill." Luckily, I was still living with my mother and didn't have the pressure of having to pay rent, so I got a job as an assistant manager at FedEx Kinko's to bring in some funds to support what we were doing. Working for Kinko's also helped in a big way because this was around 2005 before social media became popular, and we still had to rely on street teams and guerrilla tactics to get the word out on the street about the company. That meant printing out flyers, stickers, billboards, and going to clubs, and flooding the streets with our paraphernalia. So, a job at Kinko's was the perfect gig.

I got discounts on our marketing materials and things that I needed to print from Kinko's (I also knew how to trick the system so that the items I printed were so deeply discounted it was practically free.) It was a tremendous help because we could make our presence known anytime there were any significant events. I remember in high school when rappers Cameron and Charlie Baltimore first came out; they had a dope campaign that said, "Who is Cameron" and "Who is Charlie Baltimore." This was before anybody knew who they were, but you saw it everywhere, so you were intrigued to look it up and find out who these two were; we took a similar approach. We printed out flyers that said, "Who is DJ GetOnUp," since he was the one that was going to be hosting the mixtapes. We wanted his name known, so we printed thousands of these flyers with a silhouette of his logo and literally would plaster these things everywhere. Kinkos was open 24 hours a day, and I worked overnights to keep my days free. I would have one of the guys stop by the store at like 2 am to pick up boxes of flyers.

I was also looking to be innovative and tried to use email marketing to get the word out before that was even a term. There was a company that was starting called Digiwax, and they were a music distribution company. Before Digiwax, when a DJ wanted to get records to play at the club or put on a mixtape, they would have to go to the different record labels to pick up vinyl. Digiwax made it easier on the DJ by collecting the songs digitally and distributing them to the DJs via email. Once you were on their list, they would email you new tracks weekly and include the name and contact number of the A&R, manager, or executive who was working the record. Even though we weren't looking for a record deal, something told me that having the contact information of high-level executives would help us in some way, so I decided to sign up for the service. Every time I got an email from them, I would copy and paste the contact information for the executive into my database. Some notable names on my list included the legendary Jermaine Dupri from SoSo DEF, the late great Chris Lighty from Violator Management, prominent DJs, and many industry people. This list would come to help me later but let me not jump ahead.

As StreetHeat, we had great success getting our name known, making our mixtape popular, getting the attention of potential record labels, and traveling state to state to increase our notoriety. Still, internal differences started to happen within the group, and eventually, we parted ways. We all still maintained our friendship, but too many people making decisions didn't work well, mainly because we were young and had egos.

I continued to work at Kinko's, but to me, that job was just a means to an end. There was no way I was taking a step backward to stay back. It was supposed to propel me ten steps forward, so I decided to go back to banking.

Unbeknownst to me, quitting the bank to work at Kinkos then going back to the bank turned out to be an excellent decision for my career. My experience as an assistant manager at Blockbuster and my Chase banking experience combined with my sales job with AFLAC and management experience at FedEx Kinko's meant that I had a lot of professional and retail experience that would be useful for the new direction of banking.

When I started as a teller in 1999, the banking industry was service-based and relied heavily on relationship building. In the early 2000s, a switch from service to sales happened once President Bill Clinton repealed some of the Glass–Steagall Act, created during the Great Depression in 1933, and effectively separated commercial banking from investment banking to create the Federal Deposit Insurance Corporation to protect customers. The repeal took a while to kick in, but once banks could make money in more ways than they could before, they decided to open branches on every corner and treat the bank like a retail store and make money based on volume.

Because my resume had Assistant Manager positions in retail and banking positions, I was the perfect candidate for this new banking renaissance. While looking to get back into the bank, I noticed many assistant manager positions at Bank of America and decided to apply.

Hindsight is 20/20. I would have never thought that the sacrifice I made to help my friends and become an entrepreneur would come back and help me in my career. Had I stayed with Chase, it would have taken me longer than the two-year commitment I made outside of banking to become an assistant manager. On the flipside, after only a few rounds of interviews, I got the position.

I started working at Bank of America as an assistant manager, and after a few months, I got comfortable working with the branch manager, Trina Sutherland. Her and I were a dynamic duo, but like at Blockbusters, that dynamic changed when they changed leadership. Despite how well we were doing at the branch, they transferred Trina to a smaller branch right down the block and brought in a young guy named Kenny to manage our branch, which was right in the middle of Herald Square 34th St.

Kenny had no experience in banking but was a manager at Best Buy, so knowing the direction that banking was going in, it made sense why they would give him the role as a branch manager. But it didn't make sense to me; I thought, "why would they bring someone who has no banking experience to manage a bank?"

Kenny and I worked together for a few months. Still, it didn't work out because my ego wouldn't allow me to work with someone that was my age that didn't know more than me and who was making double what I was making (as the assistant manager, I had access to the P&L and knew everyone's salary).

This once again felt like déjà vu. Just like at Blockbuster when the young man took over for Edwin. In both cases, it was young men that were close to my age that I believe I had more experience than, but they were bold enough to ask for exactly what they wanted, so in turn, they got paid accordingly.

Somewhere along the line, I learned that I had to work hard for what I wanted. And even if I believe I deserved it, I had to prove myself first, then reap the rewards. The problem with that was once I proved my worth, I already gave it away for cheap, so no one was willing to pay me for what I already gave away. So now I grew bitter because I'm selling my services for half price and expecting people to pay me my worth.

So once again, instead of staying bitter and acting like a victim, I use my experience to get promoted. I started to look internally at jobs that I knew I could probably do, and I came across a position as a private banker. A private banker managed money for mass affluent customers, and so if you had investable assets starting at $250,000, the bank would assign you a banker to manage your money.

There was a team looking for a new private banker within the bank, and because I had so much success at Chase as a banker, I knew I fit the description. I applied for the position and got it and started my career as a private banker. Because I was a black banker, I wound up getting assigned to the Bronx, where the majority of the clientele were Black and Hispanic. I also had a lot of Jewish clients in areas like Riverdale and Throgs Neck. I had a book of 400 clients, and my wealthiest client was worth $22 million.

He made his wealth managing urban clothing stores, like the ones I grew up shopping at for my club outfits. While managing his money, I learned that this man owned several clothing shops on the same shopping strip; his stores had different names and technically competed against each other unbeknownst to the consumer. Learning this information made me realize how genius it was because even though the consumer thought they had a choice of where they wanted to shop from a business perspective, he controlled 100% of the market.

This mindset wasn't unique to him; I noticed this pattern with a lot of my wealthy clients. They didn't care about making a lot of money by working hard; they cared about creating sustainable businesses and systems that would make money for them whether they were around or not. Most of their companies weren't connected to them individually but more so an opportunity to meet a need of an audience that nobody was filling. My mind was expanded, and I looked at wealth differently.

Around this time, my high school friend Taqiy introduced me to a documentary called The Secret. The Secret taught a concept called the law of attraction that states that whatever you focus on will be your reality. Before this introduction, I somewhat practiced the law of attraction but never knew what to call it, so this documentary helped clarify what I knew and practiced already.

Before working at the bank, I had only read two books, but once I started realizing that my vocabulary was limited and my ability to have fruitful conversations with clients would be the difference between success and failure, I began to read newspapers like the New York Times and Wall Street Journal to learn financial jargon as well as books that would enhance my mindset. I picked up classics like Who moved my cheese, Seven habits of highly effective people, Dale Carnegie's How to Win friends and influence people, The richest man in Babylon, The millionaire next door, and one of my all-time favorites As a man thinketh. As a man thinketh was a short read, maybe about 35 pages, but it was the secret before The Secret.

In the same year that I was introduced to The Secret, for my birthday, Amina took me to Akwaabaa Mansion, bed and breakfast in Brooklyn, as a birthday gift. We stayed for the weekend, and one of the things in the room was a small book of quotes. It was 365 pages, and each page had an explanation of the quote as inspiration for the day.

After reading this book, something told me that spreading positivity was what I needed to be doing, so I started a newsletter called the Daily Word that I would send every Monday through

Friday at 6 am to my email list. Included in that list were the names I gathered as I was working on StreetHeat. I originally started with about 50 people on my list, and again it included some legends like Jermaine Dupri, Keith Murray, and a handful of DJs and A&Rs.

One DJ, in particular, was DJ KUT of St. Louis. At the time, he was the DJ on one of the biggest morning shows in New York, The Ed Lover Morning Show on Power 105. I would continue to send messages daily, but on one particular morning, I sent a daily word that would get DJ KUT's attention. It was December 23, 2006, the morning that DJ Carl Blaze was killed. I didn't know Carl, but this message was so much in alignment that you would've thought I did.

After that day, DJ KUT sent my message to everyone on his list every day, which was over 10,000 celebrities, DJs, and music industry folks. It got to a point where if he didn't send the message to his list, people would stalk me asking where it is. This was around when Twitter started getting off the ground, so my following grew significantly. DJ KUT was a big part of getting me known in the entertainment world, which would later springboard my career as an author, speaker, and financial educator.

At the Bank, I did well as a private banker; My clients loved me, and I was good at having them bring in their other assets from other financial institutions (which was one of our main goals.) I was excited about reaching my goals as a private banker because that meant getting bonuses which were very necessary. After all, Amina and I got married, bought our first home together, and expected our first child. Yup, all at the same time and in that order.

Even though I was the banker, Amina was always more financially astute than I. Originally, we were going to get married in Jamaica as a destination wedding. Still, as we started to add up all the expenses, she said it didn't make sense that we spent so much money on a wedding while still renting an apartment. She suggested we go to the justice of the peace to get married and use the money as a down payment for a home.

Since this was our first time buying a home, we took advantage of the FHA loan that only required us to put 3% down. I also took advantage of my employee discount at Bank of America, so we minimized closing costs.

I stayed at BOA for about a year, but my role became more difficult as leadership changed. The manager I had, in the beginning, knew how tough of a market the Bronx was, so the numbers that I was bringing in were better than anybody had ever done in my position. My manager knew it and didn't pressure me too much. When my new manager came in, he didn't see it this way, and because he was new to the company, he held everybody to the same standard. I'm not making any excuses, but how could I have the same goals as my counterparts who manage money on Fifth Avenue? It just didn't make sense, so just like before, I decided to promote myself and leave Bank of America and go back to Chase.

This time I entered into a leadership development program that trained assistant managers to become branch managers. Chase started this program after buying Bank of New York and turned all of those branches into Chase branches. These were locations that Chase never had a footprint in, so they had to treat them as brand-new branches.

Their mission was similar to Bank of America, in which they were hiring young people to run these branches and take them to the next level.

The program began with training for about two weeks, then a rotation of shadowing other managers at different branches until they think you're ready for your own branch. The typical program attendee rotates to different branches for six months - 1 year before getting their own branch. My first position was in Scarsdale, NY. I worked there and shadowed a manager for maybe about two months.

Keep in mind that I started my career at Chase, so I already knew many of the things they were teaching us during our training, unlike most of the other managers who entered the program and were brand new to the system.

This gave me an advantage that I gladly exploited. Within two months of the program, I was able to get my first assignment which was managing a branch at Yonkers station in Yonkers, NY. I was there for about three months then transferred to another branch in Tuckahoe, New York. While at Yonkers Station, I trained the assistant manager and tellers to ramp up their numbers quickly, and since the assistant manager was there for a while, they decided that he could continue to run the branch. At the same time, they pulled me and put me in a branch that needed more help.

The Tuckahoe NY branch was in a quiet town with about 2000 people, and 10% were black. There was a Wachovia bank next door to us that most people in the community have been banking with for many years. This became a challenge because getting a small town of people to transfer to a new bank was very difficult, but I had something to prove.

Instead of waiting for the business to walk in, I devised a plan to take advantage of our bank at work program. I learned from my days at Bank of America's private bank that even though I was in an almost impossible position, the higher-ups will always hold you accountable to the goals that they set regardless of the circumstance. So instead of running, I decided to face the challenge and make it work.

The bank at work program was a program that allowed bankers to go into where people worked and offer them bank accounts and other services instead of them having to come to the branch. Because my branch was so slow with foot traffic, I could afford to take my bankers out of the branch and leave maybe one or two people to manage the flow of the foot traffic. We killed it. Even though I was the manager and wasn't technically responsible for selling, why let my excellent selling skills go to waste? So instead of walking into people's places of business like "hey I'm the manager," I was just one of the staff ready to help clients open accounts. This gave my bankers incentive to outdo me because I didn't get paid commission on the accounts that I opened, turning my applications into bonuses for those who opened more accounts or got us another employer that we can visit. We went everywhere. I remember sitting in the lobby of IKEA in Red Hook, Brooklyn opening hundreds of accounts while our branch was in a whole other county.

Immediately we exceeded every single goal they gave us at that branch, something that it never did in its two years of existence and something that the powers that be thought would never happen. I was the last hope. If I couldn't make it work, they planned to shut down the branch.

After a year of blowing up my numbers, I started to gain so much confidence in my abilities as a branch manager that I needed a bigger challenge. I had a great team that I taught my system to, so we maintained our level of success without me being fully involved. One of my primary goals was to go back to a community where the people look like me, so when an opening at a brand-new branch in Co-Op City in the Bronx became available, I immediately threw my name in the hat.

My experience was so perfect for this position, and when I interviewed, the district manager and area manager knew that I was the guy that could take this branch to where it needed to go. This was when politics started to kick in. I was doing things at the Tuckahoe branch that were never done before. I started carrying the whole district with my numbers. Plus, because my branch became self-sufficient, my district manager would use me to jumpstart other branches in our area. If a branch were falling behind, they would have me go there for about a week to train the staff and show them my methods. Many managers didn't like this because here comes this young 27-year-old running around like he runs the place, teaching them how to do something that they probably were doing for 10 to 20 years.

Either way, that was my role, and no master, I mean boss in their right mind, would give me up. Chase had this rule: to transfer to a new branch internally, you had to be there for at least two years. Technically, since I was hopping around to different branches, I reached that limit, but I had been in my position for less than the allotted time in the system. So when it came to getting the job at Co-Op City in the Bronx, I was denied.

The district manager from the Bronx location was very upfront with me; she told me that my current bosses were being territorial and wouldn't release their best guy even though they could with a stroke of a pen.

The problem was that because Chase was investing so much money into this new branch, $8 million to be exact, they had to find somebody to run it ASAP, so time was of the essence. I thought hard about getting the position without trying to burn any bridges but couldn't think of anything.

This was a perfect position for me because I lived 10 minutes away, and I would help serve a population that I was passionate about serving. I didn't know what I was doing at the time, but instinctively, I would drive every day by the new branch, envisioning that I would be the manager when it was fully built. They were building this branch from scratch, and the location was an old gas station, so I watched it go from dust to a brand new freestanding building for months.

I had given up the fight in my logical mind, but subconsciously I still had some shreds of hope. My daughter was just born, so being close to home was so important to me. A few months had passed, and I accepted that I wouldn't be managing this branch and would make the best out of my situation at Tuckahoe. "Out of nowhere," I get a call from the district manager in the Bronx telling me that I got the branch. I couldn't believe what I heard, especially because I was told that there was no way it would happen.

Come to find out that this branch was such an important project in the region that when the regional manager asked why they couldn't find someone to manage the branch, the district and area manager told the story about how they found someone perfect. Still, because they weren't in their position for two years, they couldn't transfer out.

As fate or energetic alignment would have it, the regional manager was an old friend. Her name was Christine Lawton, and she was the district manager back when I was a banker and was responsible for approving my salary increase when Edwin allowed me to interview at Citibank. When she heard it was me, I would assume a few things ran across her mind; 1) She knew that I got busy and would be an excellent fit for this branch, and 2) She knew that if I wasn't given what I wanted, it would be a matter of time until I jumped ship and got what I wanted somewhere else. This worked in my favor, and she signed off for me to manage the Co-Op City branch.

Just like before, I hit the ground running. I believed in my ability to meet any goal I was given, so I was more than up for the challenge. I didn't get to pick my team except for one teller that I bought with me from Tuckahoe. Ricardo Basora was a young kid from Yonkers that reminded me of a young me, so I wanted to take him under my wings. There was something in him that told me he would be great.

When we got to Co-Op City, I was blessed to have a team just as hungry as I was. Before the branch could even open its doors, we were killing it. I used the same tactics at Tuckahoe at this branch, but it was with more prominent employers this time. I would also set up a table at the Stop & Shop supermarket right across from the branch and get many people to sign up since the new branch would be convenient for them.

As the branch finally opened, we maintained the same level of success and always exceeded our numbers. Still, if you understand corporate America, you know that sometimes shining too bright can be a gift and a curse. When you do the impossible, then do it twice; they think it's easy and make the impossible your norm. So, while I was proud that I was going above and beyond and exceeding my numbers, the powers at the top thought that I wasn't being challenged enough; they started to increase my goals to impossible levels. These goals were frustrating because, unlike my sales reps, I only got paid a commission if I met my branch goals. My staff got commission based on what they sold, so there were many situations in which my bankers were getting paid more than me. Despite my frustration, I still enjoyed having the ability to teach financial literacy to the community. This resulted in me doing workshops teaching the children in the community how to be better stewards of their money. After facilitating these workshops, I learned about my passion for teaching financial literacy or financial empowerment. I had volunteered with an organization called Operation Hope, teaching finances in inner-city schools, which I loved. Still, I always had the vision to not only teach children but to teach the whole community. Doing financial empowerment workshops in the community was a critical mission to me because whether it was students, young adults, professionals, or the elderly, my approach was to help a community that was not used to talking about money open up and have the necessary dialogue that it would take for us to move forward.

When I went to these workshops, I would hear the same questions: "How can I learn more? What book should I read? Who out there can guide me?" Because I was technically still a banker working 60 to 70 hours per week, I had little time to take on the community as clients. I wasn't entirely confident in the nonprofit organizations that existed. So, I decided to take matters into my own hands and write a book that spoke specifically to my community. The book was also going to be my exit strategy since I started to realize that the bank and I didn't align when it came to the best interest of my community. This was late 2008 at the height of the Great Recession and part of why they kept trying to increase my goals. Financial institutions started to panic, and those at the top didn't know what to do, so they pressured us to do the impossible by any means. I would have conversations with my friends at other banks, and they were going through the same thing.

Teaching my community financial empowerment felt more ethical, and the result of success would lead to families breaking generational curses and creating generational wealth. At the time, the only financial experts that existed on a mainstream level were Dave Ramsey and Suze Orman, and since I was a hip-hop head, I knew that there were other older hip-hop heads that I can relate to that wanted this message. There was one caveat about me writing his book... I was a licensed employee for JP Morgan with my 6, 63, and life and health insurance license, so I had to have permission from the bank to conduct any outside activities, a.k.a. start another business. So, in typical Ash fashion, I decided that I would ask for forgiveness, not permission.

I began writing my first book in the parking lot of the branch. Every morning I would leave at least two hours early, get to the branch parking lot and sit and type on my BlackBerry (Yes, this was before iPhones and Androids took over.) I did this for eight months straight and knocked out my book and was ready to share it with the world.

In high school, because I was always hustling and had money, I was nicknamed Ash Cash, so I knew if I came out with a book and the author's name was Ash Exantus, the bank would find out quickly, but Ash Cash... They'll have no idea. It was also a catchy name for a hip-hop financial expert, so I decided to release my first book under Ash Cash and decline to put my picture on it. Mind Right, Money Right: 10 Laws of Financial Freedom was my updated version of Think and Grow Rich by Napoleon Hill. I read that book every year and loved the principles, and through my experience in the private bank, I knew that money was about mindset, so it was only fitting to let that be the first message I share with my people.

The title came to me quickly because I'm a big Jay-Z fan and would always listen to my favorite Jay-Z songs on repeat. One day Mind Right, Money Right by Memphis Bleek ft Jay-Z came on, and the song stuck in my head... I got my mind right, money right, ready for war... mind right, money right, ready for war... mind right, money right, ready for war... and then it just hit me... yeah, you need your mind right to get your money right so you could be ready for W.A.R.... the Wealth Accumulation Rules! (I love acronyms). This was the original name of the book I came up with, but after further research, I decided to follow the path that most authors were following.

I was hesitant to put the book out but did so anyway and immediately started to figure out ways to promote it to reach the masses. By this time, my popularity in the hip-hop world had grown because of the daily word. DJ KUT sent it out to everybody on his email list, which was over 10,000 people. Jermaine Dupri and Chris Lighty also liked my words and started to repost my daily quotes on Twitter. As time went on, people would reach out to me for interviews and articles about money, so I used this traction to get my book on everybody's radar when it was time to put out my book.

In a strange turn of events, my boss at Chase was married to an executive at a Black bank called Carver Bank. Carver was the oldest Black bank in the country and had been around for 60 years, with its headquarters located in my hometown of Harlem, NY. The CEO at the time was looking to turn the bank around and make it more competitive with the other commercial banks that we're popping up all over the place. To do this, she hired my boss's husband, John, to head up this new renaissance. John was a former executive at Chase and had major success turning underperforming branches profitable.

My boss at Chase disagreed with how the company was increasing my goals and essentially punishing me for being successful, so she set up a meeting for me to meet with her husband to see if he could recruit me to help with his Carver bank initiative. In full transparency, I found it weird that my boss would give up her best guy, but we were all stressed during this time, and I believe that she could feel the shift in my energy and wanted to preserve my passion for helping my community.

My first meeting with John was fantastic. I immediately saw the vision for the bank, and he immediately saw my passion for my people. This combination was a match made in heaven. He had the experience, and I had the drive to make this mission work. I wouldn't be reporting to John directly, though; I would be managed by another Chase-Expat, Dennis, who I coincidentally knew from when I was a teller. We never spoke back then, but I knew who he was because he was in charge of our Bank at Work program. At 28 years old, I officially decided to leave a big Bank and take my talents to the people. This decision was the equivalent of going to a D1 school playing basketball and deciding to leave to play at an HBCU instead.

The first branch I worked in for Carver Bank was in downtown Brooklyn at the Atlantic terminal, one of the newer branches. I was tasked with doing the same thing at Chase, building up a failing branch with low foot traffic, but this time with fewer resources. Chase was a Trillion-Dollar company with branches in almost all 50 states, so they had the resources and a marketing budget to make banking with them attractive. Carver, on the other hand, had to appeal to new customers based on its history, purpose, vision, and who they were.

I did well there for a few months, but eventually, I was transferred to the main office on 125th St. This was a big deal because that branch had assets of over $150 million, and this was where all the executives sat, including the CEO. I had a big personality and was very successful at this branch, but I would bump heads with my direct manager because he found out that I was Ash Cash and thought it was a conflict of interest. I honestly believed that he was using the rules at Chase and tried to make them fit at Carver, but that was a big mistake.

The truth was that my being Ash Cash was beneficial because I started writing for Don Diva magazine and had a few features on AllHipHop.com. I was interviewed repeatedly on Hot 97s Street Soldiers with the legendary Lisa Evers, so collectively, millions of people throughout the tri-state and nationwide knew who I was. If we played it the right way, we could've used that popularity to bring in business for the bank.

Regardless of how it went down, I decided to hand in my resignation, and this was two weeks before my 30th birthday. Because of this, I decided to go out big! I rented out the 40/40 club and threw myself a retirement party. I was lit! All my friends, family, and co-workers came through to celebrate this milestone. Since I was getting all this notoriety, I decided to entirely focus on being Ash Cash 100% of the time.

I had some money saved up, but that's OK because I knew in my heart that my business was about to take off. My daughter was two years old at the time, so being pressured to quit my job while living a six-figure lifestyle might've not been the best decision to make, but entrepreneurship fell right, so I went with it. I continued to get some great looks in the media for being a financial expert and author. Through the help of Greg, I was able to land a contract with Children's Services to teach financial literacy to foster care kids that were about to age out of foster care.

The contract was pretty sizable, which was great because it allowed me to make half a year's salary working ¼ of the time, which gave me time to work on my entrepreneurial endeavors. It was the perfect storm. The one thing that I didn't anticipate was that even though I was making good money from this contract, it wasn't enough. The speaking business was cyclical, so I wasn't making a lot of money during the summer days, which meant that if I didn't have other work to supplement my income, I couldn't make ends meet.

Eventually, making five figures as an entrepreneur and living a six-figure lifestyle caught up to my family and me. We couldn't afford our mortgage, and my car note was late, so the bank and the repo man came knocking on the door, wanting to come to get the house and the car. We were forced to put the house up for sale as a short sale to avoid foreclosure, and we had to hide the vehicle inside of the garage to prevent it from being towed. This was the most embarrassing time of my life. Not only was I on radio teaching about financial freedom and had a weekly column on AllHipHop.com that had a reach of 7 million unique users per month, but my advice was also being distributed nationwide by Don diva magazine via my #AskAshCash column, and this financial expert was going broke… and it was public record.

To add insult to injury, because I had thrown myself a big retirement party, I had to suck up my ego and put some feelers out there to see what kind of work I could get. Being one that never really gives up, I decided that at this point, I needed my book to sell more, and without a face attached to it, it was hard to use my newfound fame to benefit me financially. So, I rereleased my book, but this time, since I wasn't working for anybody, I didn't have to separate Ash Exantus from Ash Cash, so I put my face on the cover. I wanted people to know that there was a young black man talking about money and doing it in a language that we all could understand.

The re-release did very well, and I even threw a book release talk at the Hueman bookstore in Harlem and invited all my friends and family. I had a big banner with my face on it, and the place was packed. Hueman was on 125th Street, literally four blocks from where I grew up on 129th and 8th Avenue, so the block also came out. The presentation went so well that I got many requests to speak and do other financial literacy work afterwards. My old boss, Edwin from Blockbuster, came to this event and was impressed with how I taught financial literacy. He was working at CitiBank and said that due to the bank's obligation to teach financial literacy, there was probably some money in the budget to bring me into all the different Citibank branches to teach their customers. This is because of the financial institution's CRA requirements from the Community Reinvestment Act, which requires banks to support the communities they serve.

Edwin passed along my information to his boss, and a conversation started. As I talked with his boss about doing these workshops, he found out that I was from Harlem, had experience in banking, and was great at reaching the community. So, he took a shot and said, "well, instead of bringing you in to do workshops one-off, what about becoming a branch manager at our 144th Street Branch?" At the time, they had a vacancy, and that branch was literally down the block from the projects and needed a manager who could speak to the community. They had about $45 million in assets, but most of it was institutional money deposited there by the state to help pump life back into that community.

When I weighed out the options, I said, "Hey, should I keep struggling and hustling trying to make ends meet or can I go back to work and get guaranteed money and end my looming foreclosure and provide for my family." I decided to take the position so we could get back on our feet. It turned out to be a great decision because right when I got the job, President Obama created the Making Home Affordable program, which meant that if you were behind on your home payments or about to lose your home, the bank would try to modify your home based on the current value. After modifications, If you could afford the payments, then they would let you stay. By taking this job and then applying for the loan modification, my monthly payments went from $3,000 to $1,200. This was a no-brainer because it was easy for me to afford $1,200 with a new job as a branch manager at CitiBank.

The biggest lesson I learned through going back to work was that you shouldn't rely on your physical labor to make ends meet. What I mean by this is that it's essential to change your relationship with money; instead of making money by working hard, make money by allowing your money to work hard for you. You do this by using the money you work for to buy income-producing assets and let the assets make money for you. Once I realized this, this became my primary goal going forward. Every day I was trying to figure out how to create passive income.

Around this time is when I started to envision myself as a media personality teaching financial education. A Black professor named Dr. Boyce Watkins who had his Ph.D. in finance, hosted an internet show on AOL (America Online, which Verizon bought for $4.4 billion in 2015), agreed to bring me on to his platform to interview me about my book and this first time on camera opened my eyes to how much more people I could reach with my message using video. I also met a good brother named Samson Styles, a correspondent for BET (Black Entertainment Network), and Samson was looking for someone to do an on-camera special on the Black/White wealth gap, and he reached out to me. Then through that relationship, Samson introduced me to his wife Tyese, who was working with a woman named Andrea Thompkins Holmes, who had a relationship with MSNBC and wanted to pitch me to them to do a finance show targeting our community. Once my eyes were open to these possibilities, I started to attract high-level opportunities that would later connect to make me an international financial motivator/educator.

Another special relationship that I would develop around this time was with the late great Chris Lighty. Chris is a Hip-Hop Icon and Business Legend. He was an American music industry executive who co-founded Violator, a record label, management, and marketing company, which represented hip hop and R&B artists such as Busta Rhymes, A Tribe Called Quest, Nas, Mobb Deep, Missy Elliott, LL Cool J, Noreaga, Uncle Murda, 50 Cent, Mariah Carey and Sean "Diddy" Combs, amongst others. The New York Times called him "one of the most powerful figures in the hip-hop business." Remember when 50 Cent did that Vitamin Water deal and made $200 million? Well, Chris Lighty had a big part to play in that transaction. Chris and I connected a few years back when I started the Daily Word, and he was one of the people on my list who would repost my words on Twitter; from the repost, we began to build an online acquaintance, but because he was who he was, I didn't know how to transition that relationship beyond thanking him for posting my words. I found out a friend of mine, Charlene Thomas, worked with Chris a while back and knew him personally, so I reached out to her to see if she could get me a meeting. He happily obliged, and we met at his office to discuss my vision. If you ever met Chris, you know he was a man of action, so during our first meeting, he introduced me to his staff and started connecting a few dots for me. He reached out to people at Black Enterprise about featuring me and my work; he got me a paid on-camera spot with Coca-Cola and spent hours telling me that self-curated video content was the future of the internet before Youtube's dominance today. Unfortunately, he passed away shortly after our connection, but he is forever embedded in my history and future because of what he helped sketch in my brain as possibilities.

As I still worked at the bank to make ends meet, I aspired to create an empire by staying Ash Cash. I did very well at Citibank. Again, like all the other branches I've ever been at, I started to increase the numbers and reach goals that the branch has never reached. I think outside the box, and whenever there's an issue, I always find a solution no matter what it is. In this case, the branch was busy only during the 1st and 15th when our customers received either their social security checks or public assistance. Because the branch was so slow with foot traffic during the other times, I knew that if I trained my bankers to get good at selling over the phone, we could reach many of our goals. This is precisely what we did. We got good at dialing and closing deals over the phone and met metrics that my branch never met. Because we were in a bad neighborhood, we decided to go outside of our neighborhood to get clients, but this was all done remotely.

At the same time because my branch was designated as the CRA branch. I was connected with the CRA manager, Rei Perez, who would book me to go to different nonprofit organizations and teach financial literacy. He came to one of these sessions and saw how good I was at presenting financial literacy topics, and once he learned my story, he said, "There's somebody I want you to meet."

Rei took me to Queens, where I met Bishop Mitchell Taylor; he ran a church and ran a nonprofit organization called Urban Upbound. Urban Upbound was located across the street from the Queensbridge Houses, and they served that population. If you don't know, Queensbridge is one of the largest public housing developments in the country, with 96 buildings. They offered college prep, job training, and tax prep and decided to start a credit union to rid the community of pawnshops and check-cashing places of conducting financial transactions. Once I met the Bishop and saw his vision and vice versa, he immediately identified me as a great candidate to become the Urban Upbound Credit Union CEO.

This was a gift from God because not only would this help my entrepreneurial career; it would also help the community; being from the St Nicholas houses, I understood this community very well. I decided to take the position, and at 31 years old, I became one of the youngest CEOs of a federally chartered bank. I bought a Mercedes Benz to match the title and saw how the power of intention could change your entire life in a matter of months. I was just facing foreclosure, now I'm living in a house that I could afford, I'm making more money than I was making before, I'm driving a brand-new Benz, and I'm the CEO of a credit union... look at God.

The position gave me great visibility, and the Bishop understood the power of my brand. Because of this, he was okay with me merging the two, so I no longer had to hide Ash Cash from Ash Exantus. He often had the news come to the neighborhood to highlight our community's work, and since I was media trained, he often shared the spotlight with me. NY1 News, The Daily News, The New York Post, Radio, Television; I would even get a chance to interview and meet former Mayor David Dinkins and meet and party with the current mayor at the time, Billionaire Mayor Bloomberg. The position was going well, but the truth was that because this was a small Credit Union with maybe about $2 million in assets, I was the CEO in title, but not really in function. We couldn't make many of the ideas that I had happen because we didn't have the capital to do it. To put it in context, at Carver Bank, I was controlled $159 million in assets, at Citibank, I controlled 45 million dollars in assets; so the $2 million at Urban Upbound was the equivalent of three of my clients at one of the bigger banks, and that $2million is what we had for the entire community.

After a few back and forths and realizing that my talent wasn't being used the right way, I decided to part ways and left Urban Upbound. At this point, I didn't have a job to fall back on but met my mentor and business manager, Tru Pettigrew, through my OG Big Bro Fred Crawford, who was managing MC Lyte at the time. I knew Fred from Harlem growing up, and we reacquainted when MC Lyte reached out to me to do some empowerment work. MC Lyte was introduced to me through my Daily Word, which DJ Kut was sending out to his list, and Lyte was one of the recipients. I'm giving you all of this backdrop because the power of relationships will take you far. Tru was a business manager and had a speaking bureau consisting of heavyweights like Chris Brussard, Kenny Burns, Aaron Paxton, Asha Tarry, and myself. He was also a marketing expert for some major brands, so he had great connections and knew how to connect the dots. His mentorship started as a business relationship, but eventually, he transitioned into my spiritual advisor and helped me get closer to God. It wasn't that I was away from God, but I didn't put God first. He put God first in everything. He had a flourishing career and an incredible family, and it was because he knew the power of his source.

My business as a financial educator and personality started to pick up. My connection with Tru began to yield me some paid speaking events, so I was definitely in a better position than I was the last time I decided to quit. One of the other things that helped me, and my family sustain financially was real estate. One of the things that my wife and I decided to do was turn our one-family home into a two-family, so we were able to bring in a tenant to pay the mortgage. This allowed me the freedom of not having to jump around to another job because I knew that at least the necessities were covered. So, Instead of looking for another job, I went back into entrepreneur mode.

I started looking for contracts that would allow me to sell my books and get more speaking engagements. My notoriety continued, and because of the media attention I was getting, I decided to release more books. When I only had one book, I would average about $250-$1,000 per month in royalties, so I figured I could increase that number to write more books. I did just that, and my passive income from books started to move up. I thought to myself that if I had the time to travel and focus on writing more books, I would be in a position that I wouldn't need anybody else's job. I started to look for contracts but couldn't find anything, then my brother Greg brought me an opportunity to become a financial counselor for a program called Jobs Plus. This position would be held at the Millbrook houses in the South Bronx, the poorest congressional district in the country. This was a great position because all I had to do was sit and wait for clients to come in, and I would give them a financial plan on how to manage their money.

When I wasn't sitting with clients, I was working on my business. I knew that the hood equated fame with money, so I didn't go in there telling them that I was Ash Cash because I didn't want unnecessary questions about why I was there. Also, I wrote this book called "What the FICO: 12 Steps to Repairing Your Credit." Deja Vu and the Comedian Earthquake had a show on WBLS 107.5 FM called QuakesHouse, and they would invite me every Tuesday to give money advice. WBLS was a legendary station in New York. In fact, WBLS (Home of the Steve Harvey Morning Show) is the second-largest urban station in NY that touts itself as the #1 source for R&B. Needless to say, a lot of people tune into this station. One day I was on the show, and one of my co-workers just happened to be listening, and she said, "That sounds like the guy that works at my job." Well, she Googled me, and my spot was blown. She came in the next day and started telling everybody that "hey, this is Ash Cash, check out his website, look at his books, he's famous." This breaking news didn't affect my job the way I thought it would; It allowed the customers to treat me with a great deal of respect and they now trusted my advice more.

When I first got there, a young black guy, William Blair, ran the program and he was intrigued with what I brought to the table, so this was a match made in heaven. But just like every single job I've ever had, leadership changed, and it was time for me to go. As I write this, I realize that I've always had a problem with a change of authority. The truth is I don't like people telling me what to do, so when I get a job, I swallow my pride and get comfortable being uncomfortable but to do it twice knowing that a change in leadership means I have to prove myself to a new person never sat well with me. This was when I realized that I was unemployable. I wasn't made for the politics of having to make someone like me in order for me to keep a job. Just pay me my worth and value, no more, no less.

This position at Millbrook Houses also started to deteriorate my well-being. Because there was a lot of gang activity, and I saw poverty every day, these conditions began to seep into my subconscious. My goal was to help solve the problem but being in that environment made me think less of myself, so it was time for me to go. I now understood why Jay-Z said, "I can't help the poor if I'm one of them" It wasn't that you couldn't or shouldn't help the poor, but if you're poor, then how can you help? Poverty and riches don't start in the physical; it begins in the mind so being amongst the poor minded couldn't help you, so I needed to get back into a rich environment to be of more assistance to those I wanted to help.

Once I left that job. I stayed on my entrepreneurial grind but also wanted to give back to my community. So, I decided that I wasn't going to be altruistic on an everyday basis. Still, I would volunteer once in a while, so I jumped on board as a World of Money Financial Institute teacher, teaching 10 to 12-year-olds how to be fiscally responsible every summer. At this point, speaking and making money as an author has now taken over my lifestyle, and I'm making enough money to make ends meet.

Amina and I were expecting our second child, so my focus was to continue to crush it as an entrepreneur to continue to support the family. Amina worked, but just like me, she would constantly leave jobs in search of her entrepreneurial journey. While we've always been able to meet our necessities, money to build stability was always an up and down type of situation. Also, to be 100% transparent, Amina and I had big dreams and wanted our lifestyle to reflect this, so "making ends meet" is relative. Collectively we were making over six figures, but that wasn't enough for the lifestyle we chose to live. It wasn't really about the money; it was that we had to work so hard for it that we didn't have time for anything else. We aimed for true financial and time freedom to allow us to do what we love instead of working for money. After our son, Ash J. Exantus Jr., aka AJ, was born, we focused more on reclaiming our time, and we knew that if we can gain enough money to buy some assets, we can get our time back.

This would be the case when I got an opportunity to become the Head of Financial Education for a new Fintech bank named BankMobile. This opportunity would further help propel my career as a Financial Educator and change my financial life forever. With my position, I was responsible for leading BankMobile's mission to financially empower every one of its over 2 million customers, students from over 800 partner universities, and school administrators through financial education. I was also in charge of recruiting and retaining students for its BankMobilist program, designed to help college students build the marketable skills they need to advance and prosper in the real world. A $10 billion dollar Bank backed BankMobile, so the visibility that this position gave me put me at the forefront of financial education. I was featured on every media outlet you can think of; from New York Times to Wall Street Journal, Forbes, Black Enterprise, Glamour, Today, CNBC, Fox Business News, US News & World Report, and even had recurring interviews on live TV with the Pix11 morning news. Even though with these interviews I was representing BankMobile, I've been told many times that my energy is infectious, so once readers or viewers were exposed to me, they wanted to connect with Ash Cash further, and that grew my brand bigger.

This notoriety would avalanche into massive book success when I decided to release my book "The Wake Up Call: Financial lessons learned from 4:44 + a Step by Step Guide on How to Implement Each Financial Principle" inspired by Jay-Z's 4:44 album. Because our primary target market with BankMobile was the college market, I was always trying to figure out how to make my message more relatable and reach students at their level, so I often tried new approaches. My friends Lenny Williams and Jeff Dess had a company called Trill, or Not Trill, and they used pop culture to teach leadership principles. From Beyonce's Lemonade and how it met the Social Change Model, to Using Marvel characters as case studies for career development, Kobe Bryant Leadership Types, How to retain college students using Kevin Durant as the example, Kanye West & The Art of the Impromptu Speech and so on. I loved how this approach resonated with the students, so on June 30, 2017, when Jay-Z dropped his acclaimed album 4:44, I immediately found how I can do the same thing with financial education.

After Jay-Z and Solange had their infamous elevator fiasco, everybody and their grandmother wanted to know the cause and whether the infidelity rumors were true. 4:44 answered those questions unequivocally, but truthfully that was only 20% of the album. The other 80% was Jay-Z giving us the blueprint to generational wealth. Lines like; "I coulda bought a place in Dumbo before it was Dumbo For like 2 million... That same building today is worth 25 million... Guess how I'm feelin'? Dumbo" that was teaching us to be more responsible with money and understanding the power of asset appreciation. Or how about, "What's better than one billionaire? Two. 'Specially if they're from the same hue as you," teaching us the power of cooperative economics. Other powerful lessons in the album included F%#K Living Rich and Dying Broke, Forfeiting the v12 Engine, Credit... That's How They Did it, Merrily Merrily Eating off of Streams (Multiple Streams of Income), Dying over the Neighborhood we don't own, Taking Chances over Advances, and Generational Wealth being the key amongst other millions of dollars' worth of game that we got for $9.99.

Seeing Jeff and Lenny successfully turn pop culture into college lessons inspired me to do the same, so I created a talk based on 4:44, breaking down the wealth principles in the album. The talk did so well that I decided to turn it into a book. My timing was impeccable because Jay-Z was up for 8 Grammys with that album, so he dominated the news cycle when my book was released. Because BankMobile was such a force in the Fintech world and their publicist solidified me as a financial expert, many media outlets saw this as historical that a "financial expert" would use Hip-Hop to teach financial literacy.

Many mainstream media outlets covered my book, from Money Magazine to Yahoo Finance, Google, Billboard, Black Enterprise, and many others. Believe it or not, the popular Hip-Hop sites took notice after, but still showed immense love, from Rap-Radar to Hip-Hop DX, The Source Magazine, Complex, HotNewHipHop, AllHipHop, and others. This level of coverage made my book take off to levels I hadn't seen yet as a self-published author. Within a week, I pre-sold 2500 copies and would sell close to 20,000 shortly after. This book turned Ash Cash into a Hip-Hop Finance Leader. The book got so big that I was even able to get an interview inside the RocNation building with Memphis Bleek, Brian Axelrod, and Jay-Z's nephew, Rel Carter, for their D'ussé Friday Podcast. This success even scored me some points at home because my hobby was now becoming a profitable business.

With success (the way we defined it) finally at our doorstep, a series of events would set us up for the next phase of our journey. Amina and I were navigating life as best we could; as parents, as life partners, as entrepreneurs, and as spiritual beings. As we stayed occupied with the different moving parts of life, our son's doctor would give us some news that slowed us down immediately. During his two-year-old visit, the doctor noticed that AJ was still babbling like an infant and wasn't as attentive to the sound of his name and other words as he should have been. He was born in 2015, and around the time of his birth, there was much coverage on Autism and how vaccines could be the cause, especially in boys. We also had a neighbor who was a member of the Nation of Islam, and they were running an Anti-Vaccine campaign, so we were constantly being informed on the potential dangers of Vaccines. In 2016 our neighbor showed us a documentary called Vaxxed: From Cover-Up to Catastrophe, which made a compelling case for staying away from vaccinating our children, specifically AJ, since he was just born. I can't say whether it was willful blindness, skepticism, or the fact that we had vaccinated our daughter TJ with no complications, but we went ahead and let the doctors give AJ all of his scheduled shots. As a believer in the Law of Attraction, I know that energy flows where attention goes. Because Amina and I had Autism in our consciousness, we inadvertently became energetically aligned with the disorder. At this particular Dr.'s visit, AJ's doctor asked that we take him for some tests. He was indeed diagnosed with moderate to severe autism.

We were fortunate that our doctor recognized the signs early, and we were not in denial or wanting to dismiss it as him just developing at a slower pace because he is a boy. Instead, we took action immediately to get AJ therapy. We arranged to have a speech therapist, occupational therapist, and an ABA therapist do home visits daily to help get AJ on track. After finding out his diagnosis, I started working from home to be available for AJ's sessions, and strangely enough, his diagnosis was the slowdown that I needed to gain more balance in my family life. Thankfully by the grace of God, after a series of treatments over two years, his diagnosis decreased from moderate to severe to mild to moderate.

I believe that EVERYTHING works for our greater good, so if you start to piece your life together, you'll notice how a few seemingly separate sets of circumstances all come together to give you something you've asked for; I didn't imagine in a million years that my "ask" for family balance would start with my son's diagnosis then result in me reconnecting with my father permanently.

I've kept in contact with my father throughout the years, and I would even take my daughter to see him from time to time in New Jersey, where he lived just so that he would have a relationship with one of his grandkids. See, despite my father having many children, out of the seven of us, I was the only one who maintained a relationship with him. My brother and sisters have their reasons for their disconnect, but for me, I never held a grudge for him not being there. As I looked at my current life and how blessed I was, I realized that him not being in my life was a blessing, so how can I curse the very blessing that has made me who I am.

My father lived in a basement apartment with a couple in Jersey City, New Jersey, for over 17 years, but the owners were getting a divorce, so he had to leave. He found a place in an apartment building and shared a two-bedroom apartment with a young Haitian lady in her 30's. It wasn't the safest if you know anything about Jersey City, especially for someone my father's age. He was pretty frugal, so his bank account was healthy, and as a guy with a big heart, he would always give to others. He made a mistake by showing kindness to his roommate, and once he opened that door, she tried to take advantage of the situation.

My father picked up on it very quickly and decided to shut it down, and in response, his roommate became a nuisance. She started to play loud music in the house, and at crazy times of night, she would bring in strangers and make it uncomfortable for somebody in their 70s. One day he called me and said, "Ash, I need you to come get me." He said, "I have money to get a new place. I just need you to help me find it and I just need you to help me move." I decided to scope out his living situation before we made any drastic moves, and the moment I got there, I realized that he had to go. This was a bad neighborhood to the 10th power, and there was no way I was going to allow my pops to be in that environment another night. So the same day I visited, I rented a moving truck, grabbed one of my friends, and loaded all of his things inside the truck, and decided that he would temporarily stay with me and my family at my house until I found him a place. My wife agreed, and we moved my dad in with us.

What started as a temporary situation wound up becoming permanent. Our home was a two-bedroom with an unfinished attic, the size of the whole house, so after my son, AJ, was born, my wife and I decided that we were going to redo the attic and turn it into two bedrooms; One for my daughter and one for my son. My daughter's old room would become a home office, but instead, we gave that to my pops.

- With my pops living with us now and Amina also opting to work from home, I started refocusing on my career. I'm currently making good money selling books, making better money as a speaker, and traveling from state to state. My work was not dependent on my location since I traveled so much, so truthfully, living in New York with its high cost of living wasn't necessary. One day, as I was taking my daughter to school, a young black guy was going from door to door, speaking to all neighbors. He had a nice suit on, and I thought he was a politician running for some office, so instead of just driving off, I waited till he got to my house to hear what his spiel was. He was not a politician; he was a real estate agent, and he said, "Hey, are you thinking about selling your house?" I immediately said no; he said, "Well, if you ever change your mind, or you know someone who is selling please let me know." I said, "cool, will do," but he didn't let up. Without being too pushy, he rebutted and said, "what if I could get you top dollar for your house would you sell?" I thought about it, and my initial answer was no, but in the back of my mind, I said, "I wonder how much money we could get for this house?" After I dropped my daughter off at school, I went back and spoke to Amina and said, hey, "here's this guy's card. He said he could probably get us top dollar for this house." Amina said, "Hey, I would love to know what this house is worth, now that we've added two extra rooms to the place." With that in mind, I called the gentlemen back and told him that I wanted to see how much we could get for the house, so I allowed him to list it.

When we bought the house initially, it was for $425,000, but then, because of the great recession of 2009, the home's value went down tremendously, and we lost most of our equity. As the economy started to rebound, we wanted to see whether we could price the house at a ridiculous amount, not sell it, but see what offers came back based on the new additions and renovations we made. After listing the home for an above-market price, our real estate agent returned with an offer that exceeded what we asked for in six days. Yes, we got someone to pay what we thought was a ridiculous price, but they saw value in our place.

Now it was time to make a decision; Amina and I looked at each other and were surprised that somebody would be willing to buy the house at that price, so we started contemplating whether we should stay or sell. At this time, I had a vision of being on television as a financial expert, and I had applied for a master's program in journalism to get my foot in the door. I was accepted and slated to start that September, and we received this offer in July. Amina and I decided to explore our options since our incomes weren't dependent on where we lived. The two places we had in mind were Charlotte and Atlanta. We said that we would go to both places, spend a week there, and decide based on that. We went to Atlanta, spent the week, and immediately fell in love, and without any prior plans or preparation, we decided to pack it all up and move to Atlanta.

It was nothing but faith and divine energetic alignment; instead of making a logical decision like we always did, we decided that we would ONLY be guided by faith and feeling. Even though we weren't prepared to move, this felt good and felt like the right thing to do. On September 12, 2018, we said goodbye to New York and made Atlanta our home. When we got to the ATL, we stayed in an Airbnb as we searched for our dream home. After a month, we found the perfect place. It was three times the size of our home in New York, half the price, and left us with over six figures in our bank account from the sale. The business was booming; I just got booked for one of the biggest speaking engagements of my life, which was going to be with TD Jakes and Black Enterprise, then the unthinkable happened.

On March 2, 2019, at 4:35 am, my mother passed away. This may sound weird, but I remember the time because an electric shock woke me up from my sleep at that time, and 5 minutes after, her nursing home called me with the news. I felt it coming, but I wasn't prepared. I was scheduled to be on a flight that morning to see her because she felt sick earlier that week. Now instead of going to see mommy on my visit, I was planning her funeral. I was her caretaker for close to a decade, and when I decided to move to Atlanta, I never told her because I knew it could potentially dampen her spirit. She looked forward to our weekly meetings, and no matter how tired or angry her face looked while in the nursing home, the moment she heard my voice, her paralyzed face would light up with a big smile. Even though I now lived in Atlanta, I would travel back and forth to New York to ensure that I was there at her nursing home, not breaking the routine.

When she passed away, it put me in a very dark place because that was my first love, the only woman who loved me unconditionally and to whom I could do no wrong. I did my best to maintain a level of sanity, but I can't describe in words what losing someone so close will do to you. During that same month, Nipsey Hussle was killed, then the following month, one of my Big Homies from my neighborhood was killed in his apartment. Nipsey's death was tragic and hit hard because of what he meant to the culture. I never met him in person but was a fan of his work and was in the process of writing a book called ***Husslenomics*** when he passed away, and I had even reached out to a few of my music industry friends who knew him to make the connection so we could work on the book together. My Big Homie, who was killed in his apartment, hit hard for me as well. He was a gangster and a gentleman who would help my mom with her groceries from time to time. He was also an OG Blood, but he made sure that none of my friends would try to pressure me to Blood In when I was a kid. He was so smart that he would teach us organized crime and how other cultures were well balanced and not all criminals. He taught us that those who had a chance to get out of the hood should be protected at all costs, and throughout the years in the hood, he provided me with some level of protection. He never ridiculed me for being on the straight and narrow and would constantly have convos with me about my work. In a way, he and many of the other gangsters in my neighborhood lived vicariously through me. These three deaths back-to-back did something to my soul.

On the outside, I looked fine, and I tried to maintain a level of normalcy, but when I was by myself, there was nothing but pain. I've never contemplated suicide before these deaths, but afterward, I would dream about it all the time. I didn't know who to turn to, and I tried to depend on my friends and family, but they too were in pain, and I didn't want to be a burden. To make matters worse, my relationship with Amina started to get distant, and we decided to take a break as we figured out what was next. During this break, I connected with people I had no business associating with, and I started to activate an old self that I abandoned a long time ago. I did things out of character for me, and I watched my life begin to go down the drain. My daughter, who had been my close companion since birth, began to distance herself from me as well, and I felt worthless and misguided. My rise to fame continued, I was getting great opportunities left and right, and my bank account would rise to levels that I hadn't seen before, but I felt empty without purpose, and I was ready to call it quits. To say without saying, 2019 was the worst year of my life. Then Covid happened and gave me a second chance.

Before the world shut down in March 2020, I had just signed a deal with Facebook to do some diversity and inclusion work with their staff. In January, I flew to Menlo Park, CA, to do a week-long

~ 87 ~

training on their campus and booked six speaking engagements with them per month. I remember this like it was yesterday because I was literally on the plane when we all heard that Kobe Bryant died. Even though I never met Kobe in person, as a hooper, Kobe was our hero. I took this personally just like I did Nipsey. The months ahead seemed like they were going to be rough, but when Covid hit, I realized that the dark place that I was in was preparation for what the world was about to endure. Before 2019, I never dealt with anything as life-shattering as losing my mom. And at the same time, I had to deal with separation from my life partner, so my faith in God hadn't been tested at a high level like this before.

I did a lot of soul-searching, reading, praying, and talking to my ancestors. I learned about astrology, numerology, and more about my history and who I was. I learned that my name meant Solid Gift of God! Whether it's Ashley or simply just Ash, which means solid and Exantus, meaning Gift of God. Imagine if I were told that in my youth! By the very definition of my name, my purpose in life was to be a "Solid Gift of God." I now knew my assignment. I understood why I've been guided and protected and why I was unshakable. To add to that, I learned to have greater pride in my Haitian culture; I hail from a group of people that successfully and permanently banned slavery. They created the first and only free Black Republic. They could do so by holding on to our African culture and those elements of spirituality that were strategically stripped away from us during the slave trade to make us weak. My bloodline is resilient and capable of enduring anything. That knowledge of self encouraged me to learn more about my ancestry. Through DNA analysis, I learned my ancestors were from Nigeria, Benin & Togo, Cameroon, Congo, Ivory Coast, and Western Bantu people before being dropped off in Haiti.

I also renewed my faith in God and decided to submit fully and lean in on the promises the most high had for my life. I realized that the good, bad, the ugly, the up, down, left, and right were all part of the plan; that everything that I've been through in my life has gotten me to up to this point, in which I am in a perfect position to bless more lives.

In 2020, I turned 40 years old, and right before my 40th birthday, I decided that I would fast for 40 days to listen to what God had to tell me. Within those 40 days of fasting on the year I turned 40, I came up with 40 principles that I used to succeed. These 40 principles are called The Cash Advances. If you were inspired by my life story thus far and want to get to a level of maximizing your full potential, regardless of your circumstances, then take heed to the things that I say in the next chapter. If applied and overstood, you will be able to take your life to the next level. Regardless of what storm you may currently be in, I want you to know that this too shall pass, and even if you're not in a storm, and everything is all good, know that as you become obedient to what your life purpose is, your life will get greater.

Ash Cash Deposit Ticket

ⓐⓒBank	**TRANSACTION #3**
2406 8TH AVENUE APT 1A NEW YORK, NY 10027-1849	DATE *October 4, 2020*

ACCOUNT NO. **CASH ADVANCES**

One Billion Dollars

WRITE AMOUNT IN FULL ON ABOVE LINE

Ash Cash Exantus

SIGNATURE

The Financial Motivator

TITLE

DOLLARS $ │*$1,000,000,000*│

The Most High GOD

APPROVED BY

TRANSACTION #3
THE CASH ADVANCES

The following are **40 principles** that anyone can use to maximize their full potential regardless of their circumstances. After each principle, you will be given room to reflect and jot down your thoughts and given a plan to move forward.

The **40 principles** are significant because I wrote this book while fasting for **40 days before** my **40th birthday**. The number 40 also has a few significances:

Angel **number 40** is a message from your angels reminding you that you are safe, well-protected, and loved. Another way of looking at angel **number 40** is a message of congratulations from your angels on all of the hard work you have been doing to achieve your soul's mission or life purpose. So if you are reading this book right now, it is a sign from your angels that you are on the right track.

Also, in Sacred Scripture, the **number 40** signifies new life, new growth, transformation, a change from one great task to another great task, etc.

For example:

The rain of the Great Flood lasted 40 days and nights.

Moses fasted for 40 days and nights to prepare himself to receive the Law.

Moses was atop Mount Sinai for 40 days and nights receiving the Law.

The Israelites wandered in the desert for 40 years after fleeing the Egyptians.

The Manna rained down on the Israelites for 40 years.

The Prophet Elijah walked 40 days and nights to reach the Mountain of God, Horeb.

Jesus fasted for 40 days and nights to prepare for His public ministry.

Jesus Ascended into Heaven 40 days after His glorious Resurrection from the dead.

And in Islam, The Holy Prophet Muhammad (SWT) was 40 years old when he first received the revelation delivered by the archangel Gabriel.

CASH ADVANCE # 1
TAKE 100% RESPONSIBILITY FOR YOUR LIFE

"Fault and responsibility do not go together, it sucks. When something is somebody's fault, we want them to suffer, we want them punished, we want them to pay, we want it to be their responsibility to fix it, but that's not how it works… As long as we are pointing the finger we are jammed and trapped into victim mode. When you are in victim mode you are stuck in suffering… It doesn't matter whose fault it is that something is broken if it's your responsibility to fix it."

- Will Smith

To live your life to the fullest, you must first take **100%** responsibility for **YOUR** life! You can blame the government, your parents, your environment, your zodiac sign, your ethnicity, the sun, the moon, or the stars but the truth of the matter is that **YOU** are the only person that can change your life, and it is fully **YOUR** responsibility. As a kid, when I read *Message to the Blackman* by The Honorable Elijah Muhammad, the number 1 message I received was that we **MUST** do for ourselves. This is why I've always been an entrepreneur at heart. From packing grocery bags to selling mixtapes and t-shirts. Even as an employee, I adopted the "do for self" mentality, which made me valuable and promoted me many times.

You must realize that where you start doesn't have to be where you finish. You do **NOT** have to be a product of your environment—I rightly earned everything I have in my life. I never complained, never wanted a handout, just did what I had to do because it was my responsibility, and once I took responsibility for **MY life**, a strange thing happened... The help came because people saw my drive. No one wants to help someone who doesn't help themselves. Do what you can with what you have, and you will begin to see significant changes in your life.

This means taking 100% Responsibility for **EVERYTHING**! Do not hold on to resentment because of your expectations of someone else that didn't come to fruition. Give up all of your excuses and know that life is 10% what happens to you and 90% how you respond to what happens. If you are looking at your life right now and don't like your outcomes, all you simply have to do is change your responses.

CRACKING THE CODE

What do you believe is holding you back from living your best life? Write down all the things below:

_____

_____

_____

_____

_____

_____

_____

As you reflect on your answers above, remove anything that doesn't include you. Stop blaming other people. Take full responsibility.

CASH ADVANCE # 2
IDENTIFY YOUR PURPOSE

"The two most important days in life are the day you are born and the day you discover the reason why."

- Mark Twain

It took me a long time to realize this, but I believe that everyone's purpose in life is to prove God. Whether you read The Bible, The Torah, The Quran, or any other religious scripture, they all say that we were made in the image and likeness of the Most High God, which means that we have infinite possibilities. We prove God by maximizing our full potential, overcoming obstacles, and becoming our greater selves daily. Our purpose isn't attached to one thing, or it is not predestined.

Many fail to realize that no matter what we believe in, every human being has been given free will by their higher power to do as they wish with their life. God doesn't tell us what we can or can't do but instead gives us back EXACTLY what we put out to the world through the law of Karma and the Law of Cause and Effect.

We are 100% responsible for the consequences of our actions. Contrary to popular belief, God does not aim to punish us; God is here to assist us in manifesting whatever we decide to conjure up. If we ask for peace, love and happiness through our thoughts, intentions, and actions, then that's what we will experience. If we ask to live in doom and gloom based on what we decide to keep our focus on, then that wish will be ours as well.

We decide which direction our lives go, and we must recognize that we live in a world created for us by us. Give love, then get love, spread hate, and hate will come back to you, live in fear, and fear will be your companion. Whatever you decide you want your experience to be as long as you are tapped into your source, you will be guided and protected to demonstrate the power of the Most High.

Even when I didn't know it, God protected me through the people he placed around me. The good, the bad, and the ugly have all helped make me who I am. The adversity I went through isn't a trophy that I hang on my wall but instead is what makes me a credible messenger to those who were told they would never amount to anything. I love being an inspiration and motivation, so I decided that that would be my purpose. It brings me joy to inspire and motivate people to live their best life, and as someone who was told that someone from my background and circumstance couldn't live their best life, it is my pleasure to be a demonstration of how you can have anything you want regardless of what others say or think.

My purpose wasn't something I found; it was part of me from the beginning. I had to identify it and then live it. I also had to realize that I have free will to change it whenever I want. If I decide that what I currently call my purpose no longer serves me or brings me joy, then it's time to demonstrate another aspect of my life, and that's my right... And it is also yours! Choose your purpose and live it joyfully!

CRACKING THE CODE

Questions to help you explore and identify your purpose.

Instructions:

- Find a quiet, peaceful place where you will not be disturbed.

- Answer each question below, think about it, and write down what comes to mind without analyzing, editing, or judging.

- Most importantly, enjoy the moment and enjoy the process of self-discovery!

Questions:

I lose track of time when I am...

_____

_____

_____

_____

_____

_____

_____

_____

_____

_____

I feel great about myself when I'm...

_____

_____

_____

_____

_____

_____

_____

_____

If I knew I couldn't fail I would...

_____

_____

_____

_____

_____

_____

_____

_____

If money wasn't an issue I would love to spend my time...

_____

_____

_____

_____

_____

_____

_____

_____

_____

My perfect day would consist of…

_____

_____

_____

_____

_____

_____

_____

_____

Three things I love about myself are...

_____

_____

_____

_____

_____

_____

_____

_____

_____

I would regret not doing these things in my life...

_____

_____

_____

_____

_____

_____

_____

_____

If I knew I was going to die one year from today I would...

_____

_____

_____

_____

_____

_____

_____

_____

_____

_____

_____

_____

_____

_____

_____

_____

_____

_____

_____

_____

_____

_____

At my funeral, I would like to hear… (what would each speaker say about you and your life; what kind of friend, family member, colleague were you; what character would you like them to have seen in you; what contributions and achievements would you want them to remember; what difference did you make in their lives; what is your legacy?)

_____

_____

_____

_____

_____

_____

_____

_____

_____

_____

_____

_____

_____

_____

_____

_____

_____

_____

These are the things I want to change about the world to make it better… (what issues in society or on the news make you most angry, what causes do you strongly believe in or connect with?)

_____

_____

_____

_____

_____

_____

_____

_____

_____

_____

_____

_____

_____

_____

_____

_____

_____

_____

_____

_____

Recall the happiest moments in your life. What were you doing? What were the circumstances? What is the underlying theme, if any?

_____

_____

_____

_____

_____

_____

_____

_____

_____

_____

_____

_____

_____

_____

_____

_____

_____

_____

_____

_____

_____

_____

_____

_____

Out of all of my accomplishments, both big and small, I am most proud of...

_____

_____

_____

_____

_____

_____

_____

_____

These are the people who inspire me most...

_____

_____

_____

_____

_____

_____

_____

_____

What gives you the most pleasure? What makes you smile? (activities, people, events, hobbies, projects, etc.)

_____

_____

_____

_____

_____

_____

_____

_____

_____

What are you good at? What qualities do you have that you are really proud of?

_____

_____

_____

_____

_____

_____

_____

What do people typically ask you for help in?

_____

_____

_____

_____

_____

_____

_____

_____

_____

What were some challenges, difficulties, or hardships you've overcome? How did you do it?

_____

_____

_____

_____

_____

_____

_____

_____

If you could get a message across to a large group of people, who would those people be? What would your message be?

_____

_____

_____

_____

_____

_____

_____

_____

_____

What are some common themes or things you notice in your responses?

_____

_____

_____

_____

_____

_____

_____

_____

What are things you discovered about yourself?

_____

_____

_____

_____

_____

_____

_____

_____

_____

_____

_____

_____

_____

_____

_____

_____

_____

_____

_____

_____

_____

_____

_____

Review all of your answers. Take as much time as you need to think about each of your answers in depth. Ask yourself how you feel when you read your answers. Note which ones move you, and which ones make you feel alive. Now, write as many answers to the final question as you can until you feel moved, extreme joy, or are even brought to tears. Once you do this, you will know your purpose. If you need more space to write, feel free to use a separate piece of paper.

My Life's purpose is...

1. _____

2. _____

3. _____

4. _____

5. _____

6. _____

7. _____

8. _____

9. _____

10. _____

CASH ADVANCE # 3
BE CRYSTAL CLEAR ABOUT YOUR DESIRES

"Lack of clarity is the primary reason for failure in business and personal life."

- Brian Tracy

Since we all have free will to be, have, and do anything our heart desires, we must be clear about what we desire out of life to maximize our full potential. Many of us are not living our desires but are living the desires of our friends and family or perhaps what we believe society wants us to be. Because you will **ALWAYS** get what you focus on if you are not crystal clear about your desires, you can go through your whole life as a successful failure... Yup, I said it! **A SUCCESSFUL FAILURE!!** Successful in the eyes of everybody else except yourself. When I first got my job at the bank, I was excited and knew that this was a stepping stone to my next journey, but in my heart, I knew it wasn't my final destination. Despite what I knew, I kept wanting to move up the ladder because of how proud it made other people but deep down inside; I knew I wanted to be an entrepreneur. I'm not saying I regret my journey, but in hindsight, I will say that a lot of my journey was to accumulate accolades and make other people happy, not myself.

Many of us are programmed by our early childhood, which often gets in the way of what we want. Let's make sure we are not living out someone else's dream, and let's be sure that we are not settling for less than what we desire. **Abundance is YOUR Birthright™**, so anything you desire is yours without compromise. Clarify your vision and know what your ideal life looks like. Don't play Cee-lo with your life. You don't have to roll the dice and see where you land; be intentional and make your vision the biggest you can make it. High achievers **ALWAYS** have big visions for their lives and don't share them with those not on the same wavelength. God has told you what is possible, so you don't need anyone else to see your vision for you to know it's possible. **Dream BIG and BE CLEAR!**

CRACKING THE CODE

Being clear on your desires first comes from silencing the outside world's noise to allow your higher self to give you instructions. In general, through meditation, you can do many things better. You make better decisions and become certain about what experiences you do and don't want as part of your journey. Meditation also has a few mental health benefits, including greater productivity and focus, less stress throughout the day, anxiety relief, and better sleep at night. Biologically, meditation helps reset our hormones, promotes faster healing, and helps us maintain a healthy body. It can help us create longevity for a better life, strengthen our intuition, and discover our higher purpose. Spiritually, meditation can help us create greater awareness of the world around us and give us a deeper connection to ourselves and our ideal life.

Effective immediately, I want you to meditate at least once per day but ideally twice, once in the morning and again before you go to bed. Allow your meditation to release any desires that are not truly yours. Stay open and allow the universe and your energy to guide you. Below is a quick start guide on meditation:

MEDITATION 101

Here are some simple tips on how to meditate.

I - Practice Good Posture

You can choose to either sit on a chair or the floor with your legs crossed. Make sure that your spine is upright with your head up. Your mind and body are intertwined, so if you are slumped, your mind will drift. A well-balanced body equals a well-balanced mind. To straighten up, imagine that your head is touching the sky. Note: Laying in the bed or on your back is not recommended.

II - Keep Your Eyes Open (If you can)

Do your best to keep your eyes open. To do so, just lower your eyes and let your gaze be soft. Keeping your eyes open will allow you to be more present. Keeping your eyes closed is an option but doing so usually makes it more likely for your mind to drift away. Many people prefer to close their eyes so by all means do what makes you comfortable. It's a good idea to experiment with both, to see what is most effective.

III – Monitor Your Breathing

Paying attention to how you breathe is a great way to anchor yourself in the present moment. Pay attention to how your breath is streaming in and out. Don't focus too much on how you are breathing – just let it be natural. If your mind is straying, you can also count your breath which is an ancient meditation practice. On your out-breath, silently count "one", then "two", and up to "four." Then return to "one."

IV - Find a Mantra (If necessary)

In some cases, monitoring or counting your breathe may not work for you. In that case, I recommend using a mantra. A mantra is a word, sound, or phrase that you repeat to yourself to aid in your concentration while meditating. A mantra can be as simple as the sound 'rum' or the word 'love,' It can be something you are thankful for or an affirmation, such as 'I accept myself.' Sometimes choosing a sound that can be stripped of all meaning works best because it won't bring up any connotation, interpretation, or judgment when you hear it.

V – Let Your Thoughts Go

When you notice your thoughts, gently let them go by returning your focus to your breathing or your mantra. Don't try to stop the thoughts because this will just make you feel agitated and defeat the purpose of meditation. Simply acknowledge the presence of these thoughts and calmly let them go.

VI- Start with 10 Minutes…

Some people enjoy meditating for an hour, while others find that they can't sit longer than 10 minutes. When you first begin, it's important that you do what feels right for you. Start with 10 minutes and only sit longer if you feel like 10 minutes is too short. Don't force yourself to meditate longer if you are not ready to do that. Some may also find setting an alarm useful. Setting your alarm for 10 or 20 minutes will allow you to not worry about the time hence letting your mind relax.

VII – Create a relaxing atmosphere…

If possible, create a special place to sit while you meditate. Some people have created a shrine or an altar that they face during meditation. If you don't want to go that far just yet, you can start small by placing a candle in front of you or objects that have meaning to you.

VIII – Enjoy yourself…

The most important part of meditation is that you enjoy yourself. Try smiling as you meditate. Be kind to yourself and enjoy your peace of mind.

CASH ADVANCE # 4
BELIEVE YOU DESERVE
EVERYTHING THAT YOU DESIRE

"In life, you don't get what you deserve; you get what you believe, plan, and expect."

- Bill Bartmann

Y ou will never have what you desire if you don't believe you deserve it. The law of attraction is real, and it will give you **EXACTLY** what you are asking for with your energy. For those unfamiliar, the Law of Attraction is the irrefutable concept that a person's thoughts, whether conscious or unconscious, emotions and beliefs attract their experience, or simply "you get what you think about most."

If you take a moment to think about it, you will realize that your attitude towards something is the reason why you are in a particular situation, whether good or bad. If you think back to anything you've accomplished in your life, I can guarantee you that at the moment you received it, you were in the right mental capacity and were able to create that as your reality.

Think about all the things you didn't get; I can guarantee that you were thinking negatively in some way, which created that reality as well. Worry, anxiety, stress, fear are negative feelings that will not create wealth, nor will it help you obtain any goal or aspiration. In his book *Conversation with God, Neale Donald Walsh says eloquently* that **"The Universe ONLY says YES!"** This means that whatever you believe is what is going to be your reality. If you believe that you are not worth your desires, then the Universe will say **YES!** you don't deserve them, and you will never get them. If you believe that reaching your dreams and aspirations are going to be a struggle, then the Universe will say **YES!** then give you circumstances in which your dreams and aspirations become a struggle to achieve.

As you are moving in the direction of your dreams make sure you understand that you will **ALWAYS** get what you expect; expect the worst then the worst will happen, expect peace and blessings then peace and blessings will be your lifestyle. Believe that **Abundance is Your Birthright**, and you will see abundance everywhere you go.

When I was learning about the Law of Attraction and figuring out how to become a master manifestor, the biggest thing that stopped me was giving too much attention to my current circumstances instead of focusing on what I wanted. Like, how can I believe I'm rich if bills are due and my account is negative? How can I believe in wellness, when I feel sick? How can I believe in trust when I'm surrounded by backstabbers? And How can I believe in peace when I'm surrounded by chaos?...but this is the imperative key to manifestation! As Wallace D. Wattles said is his classic book, *The Science of Getting Rich*, "To think health when surrounded by the appearances of disease or to think riches when in the midst of the appearances of poverty requires power, but whoever acquires this power becomes a mastermind. That person can conquer fate and can have what he or she wants."

You **MUST** believe and focus on what you desire. Even when the evidence doesn't show this to be possible you must remind yourself that you are a walking miracle and miracles happen every day! The truth is that it is not what you don't know that is holding you back; it is what you know that isn't true that is holding you back. Meaning that you believe that you have to see it to believe it; when the truth is once you believe it, you will see it. Stop fighting to hold on to limitations taught by people who weren't in the situations you wanted to be in. How are spiritually and monetarily broken people going to tell you how to become whole? Someone who has not been able to live their dreams is not in the position to guide you on your journey.

You deserve all the goodness and greatness that the world has to offer, and the moment you accept this as your reality, you will begin attracting the life you desire.

CRACKING THE CODE

Repeat these Affirmations once a day or as many times you deem necessary to retrain your brain and accept your Abundance

- I deserve to have a great life.

- I deserve the very best in my life.

- I am capable of creating and maintaining a great life, and I'm worthy of the effort.

- I deserve and accept all of the goodness this world grants me daily.

- I know what I want, and I ask for it.

- I receive love and give love.

- I deserve to feel good.

- I deserve the best, and I accept the best NOW!

- I am always provided for according to my needs

- I deserve happiness.

- I am a Divine creation, a piece of God; therefore, I cannot be undeserving.

- I deserve to relax more and take it easy.

- I always expect miracles.

- I deserve the best, and it comes to me NOW.

- I am fully deserving of abundance, happiness, and blessings.

CASH ADVANCE # 5
BELIEVE IN YOUR POWERS TO MAKE ANYTHING HAPPEN

"Anything is possible no matter who you are, or where you come from. Find your path and stay on it, if you want something bad enough, nothing can stop you."

- Eddie Spears

Believing in your power to make ANYTHING happen will get you into manifestation mode. Once you realize how the universe works, you will understand why you need to control your negative thoughts and feelings. You **MUST** remember that what you believe will become your reality, so believe in yourself first and foremost, and believe that you have created the life you are currently living.

Even though we live in an abundant world as human beings, we tend to focus on the negative aspects of life. I used to live by the saying, "Hope for the best but expect the worst," and my rationale was that if I hoped that everything worked out and it didn't, at least I would be ready for the worst thing that could happen. In theory, this may work, but practically, it is one of the worst things we can do because the universe will ALWAYS give us what we expect. Once I recognized my power to make things happen, I got rid of unempowering words like "I Can't, I hope, or I'll try." These words are limiting and signal to the universe what type of experience I wanted to have. So, I didn't want to attract situations that I couldn't have, so I became more affirmative with my words and actions. Before I got there, I had to manage my limiting beliefs and negative thoughts.

We may think that resisting negative thoughts or limiting beliefs will get us closer to abundance, but it's the opposite; The Law of Attraction says that what we resist will persist. Instead of resisting these thoughts, I learned how to manage them up and out.

You can fight against poverty, or you can build wealth. You can either be against hate or only promote love. The Universe will give you what you are paying attention to, so as it relates to your negative thoughts and limiting beliefs, you must not fight against it, but instead, you must allow it to pass through without resistance.

CRACKING THE CODE

Below are steps on how to deal with limiting beliefs and negative thoughts:

STEP 1: RELIEVE YOUR NEGATIVE EMOTIONS

The first step to moving negative thoughts up and out is to awaken them. Get your sadness, anxiety, anger, guilt, shame, or embarrassment bubbling and stir it up inside of you. Think of the things that trigger these emotions and confront them head-on. As you are conjuring up these thoughts, make sure you are focusing on your breath. Stay present and mindful of these thoughts but continue to take deep breaths.

STEP 2: MOVE YOUR FEELINGS OUT THROUGH WRITING

Holding thoughts inside can form a mental prison. The hands, feet, and voice are key channels for releasing emotional energy from the body; that's why the best way to free yourself from these emotions is to write them down. By doing so, you connect your mind with your hands and form a powerful release. This technique is an effective way to start getting your negative thoughts out of your head, reducing its toxicity to your body, and stopping it from potentially spilling out into your everyday life.

Make sure that as you are writing down your emotions, you are doing so without judging them. This exercise is simply to help you become aware of what's going on inside you. If you judge yourself for these thoughts or edit them in any way, you are lessening the effectiveness of this method.

STEP 3: SHARE YOUR STORY

Now that you have gotten your negative thoughts out of your head and body, it's time to fully decrease its power by sharing them with another person. This may be done individually or in a group setting but just make sure it is a safe space. Sometimes, it may help to speak to someone who has no bias towards you or with whom you have no relationship. This is why a therapist, psychiatrist, or an anonymous group works effectively because there will be no judgment (whether real or perceived).

Also, finding a support group is helpful because hearing that others have similar experiences will help you realize that you are not alone. This will help shift your perspective from self-judgment to self-acceptance and begin the healing process.

Use the space below to write:

_____

_____

_____

_____

CASH ADVANCE # 6
UNDERSTAND THE POWER OF
ENERGETIC ALIGNMENT

"When you are in alignment with the desires of your heart, things have a way of working out."

- Iyanla Vanzant

According to Universal law, you cannot experience anything that you are not in energetic alignment with. If you want to live your best life, you must be in the same frequency as the experience that constitutes your best life. To put it more plainly, your life is like a radio station; If you want to listen to Hip-Hop and R&B on the radio, it is impossible to do so if you are tuned into the Country station. To listen to Hip-Hop and R&B, you must turn your radio dial to the station playing Hip-Hop and R&B. In the same breath, you can't complain about the music if you are unwilling to change the station. If you are tired of country music and all you keep doing is complaining about how bad country music is, you will be disappointed when that station NEVER plays Hip-Hop and R&B. Instead, you can simply turn the dial to what you want to listen to and become happy with that experience.

That's exactly how life works; everything on earth vibrates at a specific frequency, so if you want to experience peace and prosperity, then tune into the vibration of peace and prosperity. If you are experiencing an undesirable frequency, then you must change your frequency to what you want to experience instead of where it currently is at the moment.

The easiest way to change your frequency and become a vibrational match to what you desire is to focus on creating positive emotions of love, joy, appreciation, and gratitude throughout your day. Life will **ONLY** give you back what you put out. Be what you want to attract, allowing you to be a vibrational match to what you are being.

Never look at a negative situation and try to wish it away; just know it is in your life because you are a vibrational match. The moment you stop vibrating on the level of what's undesired will be the moment that you experience changes.

CRACKING THE CODE

Recite these affirmations anytime you find yourself in alignment with undesirable experiences:

- I joyfully and easily align with my heart's desires.
- I am aligning with easier ways to experience more abundance.
- Money flows to me easily and effortlessly.
- I welcome abundance in all forms.
- I am becoming aware of the abundance that's all around me.
- My joy is my guide.
- Life is creating beautiful, abundant experiences for me to align with.
- Life supports my heart's desires, and I am well taken care of.
- Abundance flows to me easily & steadily.
- Abundance is my birthright.

CASH ADVANCE # 7
VISUALIZE THE LIFE YOU DESIRE TO LIVE

"To bring anything into your life, imagine that it's already there."
- Richard Bach

Visualization is the technique of seeing an image of yourself that you are proud of in your mind. Envision yourself in your dream home, cooking in your dream kitchen, using your dream bathroom. Start to feel the feeling of living your best life and reaching your full potential. To take it a step further, do an actual tour of your dream home if you can, test drive your dream car, go to the lot and sit in the car, envision yourself driving it. Where will you go? Live out your dream in your mind as much as possible, then do some things in real life that coincide with living your dream.

Every promotion I've ever received was preceded by me envisioning myself in that position. In full transparency, I would even practice talking to myself in the mirror as if I were the person, I envisioned myself becoming. Remember when I received that "Random" call for that bank position I wanted in the Bronx? I used visualization to receive it. If you don't recall, I drove by the branch every day as they were building it, as if I worked there just to visualize the route and get the feeling of working so close to my home. I saw what I wanted in my mind and did what I needed to do to give me the feeling of receiving it.

Scientifically the mind doesn't know the difference between what is real and what you imagine, which is why many successful people use visualization to achieve their desired outcomes.

Elite athletes use it, the super-rich uses it, and peak performers in all fields use it. This is their secret weapon, and now it's yours to use.

CRACKING THE CODE

Think about the most important things that you want to accomplish while you're on this earth; I do not want you to look at it from the lens of where you are right now. What I want you to do is to imagine that you are getting a lifetime achievement award. During the intro of your award, the person doing the introduction will read your bio, but it will have things you could accomplish on a grand scale.

It won't talk about the kind of house you had or the car you drove, or how many vacations you went on, but instead, it will give you the tangible things that impacted the world and other people.

I believe that if you focus on the bigger picture, then the things you do day in and day out will ultimately lead you to the house, the car, the relationship, or the kids, but it starts with your purpose.

What will you accomplish when it's all said and done?

For Example, If I were given a lifetime achievement award, I would like it to read:

Ash Cash Exantus is a pioneer on the forefront of spirituality and financial education. He is a bestselling author who wrote 40+ books that have sold over 200 million copies. He sold these copies by providing the best possible book that helps and empowers anyone who reads them. He is the creator of a series of original programming that has been seen all over the world. His series helps shed light on social and financial issues. As a highly sought-after paid speaker, people come to hear him speak over and over, each time touching their hearts and moving them into action. He has a nationally syndicated Talk Show and Radio show that attracts millions of daily viewers and listeners and is instrumental in creating a dialogue for Self-Improvement. All of his business ventures provide jobs and entrepreneurial opportunities for millions of people around the world. He is the recipient of a Grammy for best Audiobook, Emmy, Nobel Peace Prize, and now this Lifetime Achievement Award... Ladies and gentlemen, put your hands together for... Ash Cash!!!! (Crowd claps)

CREATE YOUR LIFETIME ACHIEVEMENT AWARD INTRO

On the following page, create your Lifetime achievement award introduction as if you won the prestigious prize, and someone would introduce you before you went on stage. You must first create a vision and mission statement, and your ultimate vision should be aligned with these two.

Vision = End Game

Mission = How You Will Get There

Your vision statement guides your life and provides the direction necessary to live a fulfilled life.

Think of your vision statement as the roadmap to total bliss during your lifetime.

Your vision statement can be a sentence or two. For example, Oprah Winfrey's vision is: "To be a teacher and to be known for inspiring my students to be more than they thought they could be."

Your Personal Mission Statement defines how you will get to your vision. Think of the vision as the GPS, but the mission is the car (AKA the vehicle that will get you to your destination)

For example, Oprah's original mission statement was…

"To uplift, enlighten, encourage and entertain through the medium of television.

My Vision for my life is (Vision Statement):

_____

_____

_____

_____

_____

_____

I will achieve this vision by (Mission Statement):

_____

_____

_____

_____

_____

_____

_____

Use the space below to write your lifetime achievement introduction:

_____

_____

_____

_____

_____

_____

_____

_____

_____

_____

_____

_____

_____

_____

_____

_____

_____

_____

_____

_____

_____

_____

_____

CASH ADVANCE # 8
STOP DOING AND START BEING!

"Act as if! Act as if you're wealthy and rich already, and then you'll surely become rich. Act as if you have unmatched confidence and then people will surely have confidence in you. Act as if you have unmatched experience and then people will follow your advice. And act as if you are already a tremendous success, and as sure as I stand here today - you will become successful."

- Jordan Belfort, The Wolf of Wall Street

O ne of the biggest mistakes people make when wanting to live out their best life and maximize their full potential is asking what they should be doing to get to the next level, but the real question they should be asking is who am I supposed to be to get to the next level.

Visualization is the beginning process that gives you the confidence to want to live your best life, but once you get past the confidence part, the way to materialize the life that you desire it's a start now and just be.

Most people think that to become a millionaire, you must have $1 million or more in your bank account, but the truth is that you become a millionaire by your habits, not by what you have in your account. To prove this point, you can simply look at someone who wins the lottery who has not fully embraced the habits of the wealthy. On average, they lose their millions between 1-5 years. On the flip side, if you stripped a wealthy person of all of their material possessions, they would be back to their wealthy status because of who they are and the habits they have adopted that have made them wealthy.

So if we go back to the $1 million example, ask yourself who would you become if you had $1 million? What habits would you adopt, what kind of knowledge would you acquire, and who would be your circle of influence? Instead of waiting to have $1 million to become all of the above, start becoming that now.

When I was a teller, I was acting as if I was a personal banker; when I was a personal banker, I was acting as if I was a branch manager; when I was a branch manager, I was acting as if I owned the bank. Even during my entrepreneurial journey, I use the same method. When I spoke in front of 1-10 people, I would act as if I was in a room of thousands of people when I only made four figures in my business; I acted as if I was a five-figure business when I was a five-figure business I acted as if I was a six-figure business. When I became a six-figure business, I was acting as if I was a seven-figure business, and so on. Every step of the way, once you become what is necessary to attract the situation in real life, that becoming will allow you to live out your dreams faster.

CRACKING THE CODE:

Action: Faith it til you make it! Create a personal statement of what your ultimate goal in life is. Write down every detail of what you would like to accomplish, and then write it as if you have attained it already.

For example, My Personal Statement goes as such:

I am happy that I am financially free. I have gained my wealth in various amounts and in various ways.

I am a bestselling author who has written several books that have sold millions of copies. I have sold these copies by providing the best possible book that helps and empowers anyone who reads them.

I am a film producer who created video series that helped shed light on social and financial issues that have been seen millions of times.

I am a highly sought after paid speaker who receives thousands of dollars per talk. People come and hear me speak over and over, each time touching their hearts and moving them into action.

I am an Emmy Award-winning Talk Show host as well as a Radio personality on a nationally syndicated show. Collectively both shows attract millions of viewers and listeners and have created a dialogue for Self-Improvement.

I created motivational albums that have sold millions of copies via compact disc, mp3's and all other forms of digital format.

I am successful and still have time to spend with my family. I have a perfect work/life balance and a beautiful relationship with my wife and kids. My family and friends are proud of me and I help each of them fulfill their dreams.

All of my ventures provide jobs and entrepreneurial opportunities for all of the people I care for.

I believe in myself and in my abilities, with no restrictions and will continue to live life to its fullest.

As per the example above, your personal statement must be specific and include your definite purpose in life. You must list how you expect to obtain it and what you intend to give back.

Begin at once to become the person you want to be; you must walk like it, talk like it, breathe like it, dress like it, think like it. Become It!! Every morning when you wake up, you must repeat your personal statement aloud while looking in the mirror and again before you go to sleep. As you go out into the world, remember who that person is and begin to be that person immediately. As time goes on you will subconsciously start to visualize yourself being that person and as a person thinketh so shall they be!

Use the space below to write your personal statement:

_____

_____

_____

_____

_____

_____

_____

_____

_____

_____

_____

_____

_____

_____

_____

_____

_____

_____

CASH ADVANCE # 9
TAKE ACTION ACCORDING TO YOUR BEING

"People may doubt what you say, but they will believe what you do."

- Lewis Cass

As we get comfortable with being instead of doing we must make sure that our actions do not contradict our desires. Think about what you are asking for, and make sure that your actions are aligned with what you expect to receive. For example, If you are asking for a profitable business but you give away all of your products and services for free then you are contradicting your ask.

Effective immediately, you must act as if you are receiving what you desire. Do **EXACTLY** what you would do if you were receiving it today! Make room to receive what you asked for and let your actions reflect someone who has certainty that what they've asked for is on its way.

And don't worry about not fully being prepared to be that person because as you move with intention, you will realize that you are already fully equipped for the success you seek. Ask yourself, "what action steps can I take today that will move me closer to my goals?"

Then begin to take those actions. There is nothing you need to wait for you can begin taking action **TODAY**!

CRACKING THE CODE:

Regardless of where you are right now, it's time to open up your mind and your consciousness to assess what your ideal life looks like so you can begin to plan for it and take action accordingly.

Please see the tasks below to begin the process:

What does your ideal lifestyle look like?

_____

_____

_____

_____

_____

Would you be working if you didn't need the income? If so, what kind of work would you be doing? How many hours per week?

_____

_____

_____

_____

_____

_____

_____

_____

Who are you spending time with? How frequently are you seeing them?

_____

_____

_____

_____

_____

What are you doing with your free time?

_____

_____

_____

_____

_____

_____

What city and country do you live in? Is it the same place all year round?

_____

_____

_____

_____

How many weeks per year do you travel?

_____

_____

How much does it cost to live your ideal lifestyle? (Please be as exact as possible; look up the home prices where you want to live, the monthly expenses you will incur, etc;)

_____

_____

_____

Now review your answers above and jot down all of the action steps that you can take today to begin moving in the direction of your desired lifestyle:

1. _____

2. _____

3. _____

4. _____

5. _____

6. _____

7. _____

8. _____

9. _____

10. _____

Use the Affirmations Below if needed to attract Your Ideal Life:

I am increasingly confident in my ability to create the life I deserve
I am creating my life according to my dominant beliefs, and I am improving the quality of those beliefs.
I am willing to believe that I am the creator of my life experience.
I am willing to believe that by focusing on feeling good, I make better choices that lead to desired results.
I am worthy of love, abundance, success, happiness, and fulfillment.
I can do anything I put my mind to
I am successful in whatever I do
I am making things happen
I persist with confidence
I see endless opportunities before me
I'm living my full potential
I am powerfully positive in everything that I think doing say

CASH ADVANCE # 10
TAKE ACTION DESPITE OF FEAR

"When you stay on purpose and refuse to be discouraged by fear, you align with the infinite self, in which all possibilities exist."

– Wayne Dyer

Most people will gravitate towards doing what they are familiar with and staying within their comfort zones but maximizing your full potential cannot happen if you stay in your comfort zone. Those who take their lives to the next level take action despite how uncomfortable they may be. They are not perfectionists, so they do it ugly, they do it dumb, and they do it afraid. Fear is the biggest block that stops the average person, but we mustn't let that stop us.

From an anatomy standpoint, when we are afraid, our body reacts with increased blood pressure, dilated pupils, and our heart pumps blood at a higher than normal speed. But sometimes, the danger we anticipate is only in our mind and as this type of fear gets out of hand, we stop our true desires from being a big part of our existence. But what are we afraid of?

There are many types of fear; fear of failure, rejection, change and losing power. We've all heard the saying that "thoughts become things," but as we allow fear to take over our minds, we create the very situation or circumstance that we were originally afraid of. When we're afraid, we don't make decisions that are in our best interest. This is why we often make stupid decisions just so that we are accepted by society, friends, and family. Our fear of rejection is so deep that we begin to hide certain traits to be accepted and not be judged. Many of us do this at an early age. As we develop into adulthood, we become accustomed to hiding a piece of our real self and creating what French philosophers call "the ideal ego," which is a self that we create to fit our environment and not be rejected. Our ego, if not checked, gets bigger and bigger and soon we do not recognize ourselves and live a life that is not really ours.

Take the leap! Regardless of being afraid, understand that this fear stands in the way of you living out your desires. Be willing to feel the fear but take action anyway. Remember that there have been things you were afraid of all throughout your life that you triumphed through anyway.

CRACKING THE CODE:

ACTION: How to Overcome Fear in Order to Empower Your Thoughts

1. Find out What You Are Really Afraid Of

To begin to overcome your fears, you must get specific about what exactly you're afraid of. Paint a mental picture of the situation. Play it out using different scenarios. What are you really scared of? What is the root cause of this fear? Use the space below:

_____

_____

_____

_____

_____

2. Be Aware of How Your Fears Are Affecting You

Now that you have the specifics, it's time to recognize your fears effects on you and your life. We often convince ourselves that our fears are no big deal, so we go on with our lives, not realizing how crippling they can be. Thoughts become things, so you must have an awareness of what you are creating or pushing away. Answer below: How are my fears stopping me from living my best life?

_____

_____

_____

_____

_____

_____

3. Write Your Fear Down on Paper

Journaling is an effective way of getting your fears out in the open. It's important that you get your fears down on paper to begin to address them thoroughly. Trying to think them through doesn't work. They get trapped in your mind and grow bigger, eventually making matters worse. By writing them down you don't give more attention to them than necessary. Use the space below:

_____

_____

_____

_____

_____

4. Be Grateful

Whenever you feel fear, switch it over to what you are grateful for instead. Gratitude is the most powerful way to create a mindset shift and overcome fear. Take a minute and close your eyes. Put your hand on your heart and begin to appreciate everything and everyone you are grateful for. This includes the less favorable things that at first seemed "bad" or "negative" but now you realize they have taught you invaluable life lessons. Be grateful for it all because the experience is what has shaped you to be who you are today and what will continue to help shape who you become tomorrow.

5. Talk it Out

Sometimes talking out your fears with someone else helps you realize that you had nothing to fear to begin with. Because others aren't as emotionally invested in what you are afraid of, they can help you see clearer. Also, by saying it out loud, you diminish the judgment of the fear. You are living your truth, so no one can hold it against you. The only caution in this method is to make sure you do not turn talking it out into a complaining session or pity party.

6. Find a Therapist

If none of the above is working, it may be time to look for a good therapist. Therapy can be life-changing and is highly beneficial. The trick is finding a good therapist that you feel comfortable with. This is someone you will share your deep secrets with, so make sure the vibe is on point before committing to that person.

7. Try Neuro-Linguistic Programming (NLP).

Neuro-linguistic programming or NLP is an approach to communication, personal development, and psychotherapy created by Richard Bandler and John Grinder in California. The creators claim there is a connection between neurological processes (neuro-), language (linguistic), and behavioral patterns learned through experience (programming) and that these can be changed to achieve specific goals in life. This technique has been made famous by self-help gurus, including Tony Robbins. In essence, NLP helps you learn how your mind works and has helped thousands eliminate phobias, fears, and other emotional problems. Give it a try if it feels right to you.

8. Hire a Life Coach

Many people don't realize that their fears stem from fearing success or fearing failure. A goo0d life coach can help you examine what you truly want from life and guide you on how to get there. They can also help you determine where your fears come from. Hiring a life coach can be scary initially, but you will realize that they are very helpful in getting you clear about what you want and what's stopping you.

CASH ADVANCE # 11
NEVER TAKE NO FOR AN ANSWER

"The difference between successful people and unsuccessful people is that successful people do all the things the unsuccessful people don't want to do. When 10 doors are slammed in your face, go to door number 11 enthusiastically, with a smile on your face."

-John Paul DeJoria

If you want your desires, then nothing can stand in your way. From an early age, I never really took no as an answer, I always knew that no was just yes to a different question. For me no meant next opportunity. It didn't mean to stop going after what I wanted, it just meant that I probably couldn't do it with who I wanted to do it with. As my good friend Mike "Cobaine Ivory" Mcfadgen would say, rejection is protection. When something doesn't happen when you want it to happen, it could be the universe protecting you from something that you aren't even aware of.

As we stated earlier, for you to experience anything in your life, you must be in energetic alignment with that thing. If the time isn't right or the circumstances don't permit it, your desires may be delayed for a moment, but it doesn't mean giving up and changing courses.

All it means is that God is preparing something even better for you. Don't be impatient because forcing things into alignment will only push them further away from you. I remember being rejected by many media outlets when I first started my journey. I used to take it personally, but as time went on many of these media outlets have helped propel my career in ways I didn't know was possible. It was all about timing and energetic alignment. Had I forced the issue at the time, I may have burned bridges that I would need to cross later. Be patient and know that the moment you ask God for something, you will get three answers:

1. Yes

2. No Now

3. Or I have Something Better!

CRACKING THE CODE:

To practice not taking NO for an answer, you must understand that patience plays a big role. The following are affirmations for when you are feeling impatient:

1. I trust that everything will happen in its own time.

2. The Universe will give me everything I desire when it is the right time.

3. I feel at ease while waiting.

4. I am filled with patience and peace.

5. The Universe has divine timing.

6. All good things are coming to me.

7. I gently release expectations.

8. I relax and enjoy the journey.

9. I am joyful and content with my progress.

10. My heart is open to miraculous things happening to me.

11. I honor the time it takes for everything to manifest.

12. I am committed to my soul's purpose, regardless of how long it takes.

13. Everything I need comes to me exactly at the right moment.

14. My purpose drives me at exactly the right speed.

15. I trust the timing of my journey.

CASH ADVANCE # 12
EMBRACE NEGATIVE AND
POSITIVE FEEDBACK

"Examine what is said and not who speaks."

– African proverb

After you take the plunge and overcome your fears to do something you were afraid to do, you will get feedback whether you like it or not. Even if you are not afraid, once you start living out your desires, many people will give their take on what you are doing. Whether it's good or bad, ONLY use feedback to mprove. When I wrote my first book, I thought it was perfect; in fact, when I shared it with my friends and family, they loved it. It wasn't until I gave the book to one of my professors in college that I started to notice many errors in my book. I edited the book eight times before getting it right. If it weren't for my ability to accept feedback, I probably would have a poorly written book on the market that no one buys but instead 12 years later and over 35,000 books sold. My first book continues to be a source of impact and income for me.

Also, remember that your goal is to maximize your full potential, and the only way to do that is to do everything in excellence. Never be ok with being mediocre and never not strive to be your absolute best. Don't take positive or negative feedback personally; take it as an opportunity to get better and move towards your excellence. All feedback means there is room for improvement.

CRACKING THE CODE:

Take a SWOT analysis of your life and become self-aware of your full profile:

WHAT IS A SWOT ANALYSIS?

SWOT stands for

- **S**trengths
- **W**eaknesses
- **O**pportunities
- **T**hreats

HOW TO DO A PERSONAL SWOT ANALYSIS?

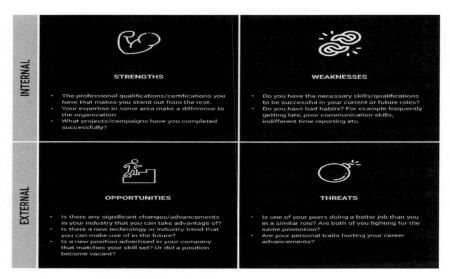

Use the space below to create your SWOT analysis

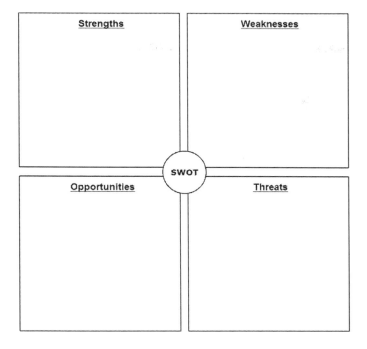

CASH ADVANCE # 13
COMMIT TO GET BETTER

"The journey is never ending. There's always gonna be growth, improvement, adversity; you just gotta take it all in and do what's right, continue to grow, continue to live in the moment."

-Antonio Brown

No matter how high I climbed on the corporate ladder, the Entrepreneurship ladder or even in my personal relationships, I always knew that I could be better than I was the day before. It wasn't about competing with anybody else, but it was about making sure I was maximizing my full potential and I was being the best version of myself. That's why it's imperative that you never stop learning. The only time you should stop growing is when you're dead, other than that, every single day you must be committed to getting better at what you do and how you do it.

What are some daily habits that you can implement in your life that can help enhance who you are? Wake up early, pray/meditate, read books, drink more water, etc; Whatever those habits are make sure you are committing to change and for the betterment of yourself. Don't try to improve all in one shot; improve in small increments and decide what to improve on.

CRACKING THE CODE

Use the below space to plan out your continued learning and improvement:

10 Books I will read this Year:

1. _____
2. _____
3. _____
4. _____
5. _____
6. _____
7. _____
8. _____
9. _____
10. _____

3 Trade Magazines I am going to subscribe to:

1. _____
2. _____
3. _____

My mentor or Business coach is:

_____

I will take these 3 online courses this year:

1. _____

2. _____

3. _____

My accountability group is:

_____

CASH ADVANCE # 14
CELEBRATE YOUR SMALL WINS

"Celebrate every win! Reaching your goal should not be the only celebration. Celebrate milestones you reach, celebrate your progress, no matter how big or small. Daily wins lead to a lifetime of success."

-Unknown

Sometimes while on your journey, you will be so engrossed in what's next that you don't take a moment to realize what's now and what you have done in the past. I remember the first time I was on the radio speaking to 2 million people and was getting calls and texts from everyone telling me how proud they were of me. Because I was so focused on the "next thing" I didn't even take time to celebrate how far I came which allowed me to downplay who I was in the world. Then I started to take to heart all of the critiques from people who didn't even really matter, not realizing that I had already surpassed my own expectations. I didn't know it because I wasn't taking score. What I had to realize was that I was the sum total of ALL of my successes.

The world will undoubtedly critique you and try to convince you that you aren't a big deal. Many times, we will critique ourselves and downplay our accomplishments. In a world where good is never enough and great gets looked down on by people who never even had that gall to try, it is imperative that you enjoy your journey and CELEBRATE YOU!!

We all have many accomplishments to be proud of but because we are so focused on the result, we have not taken the time to realize how far we've come.

It is mandatory that once in a while you celebrate yourself. Realize where you came from, see where you are now and appreciate the fact that you're moving in the right direction.

Find opportunities to congratulate, compliment and reward yourself, even for the smallest successes because in the grand scheme of things a win is a win. There are no big or small. As Oprah said, "The more you praise and celebrate your life, the more there is in life to celebrate."

CRACKING THE CODE:

Write a list of your top 100 wins.

1. _____

2. _____

3. _____

4. _____

5. _____

6. _____

7. _____

8. _____

9. _____

10. _____

11. _____

12. _____

13. _____

14. _____

15. _____

16. _____

17. _____

18. _____

19. _____

20. _____

21. _____

22. _____

23. _____

24. _____

25. _____

26. _____

27. _____

28. _____

29. _____

30. _____

31. _____

32. _____

33. _____

34. _____

35. _____

36. _____

37. _____

38. _____

39. _____

40. _____

41. _____

42. _____

43. _____

44. _____

45. _____

46. _____

47. _____

48. _____

49. _____

50. _____

51. _____

52. _____

53. _____
54. _____
55. _____
56. _____
57. _____
58. _____
59. _____
60. _____
61. _____
62. _____
63. _____
64. _____
65. _____
66. _____
67. _____
68. _____
69. _____
70. _____
71. _____
72. _____
73. _____
74. _____

75. _____
76. _____
77. _____
78. _____
79. _____
80. _____
81. _____
82. _____
83. _____
84. _____
85. _____
86. _____
87. _____
88. _____
89. _____
90. _____
91. _____
92. _____
93. _____
94. _____
95. _____
96. _____

97. _____

98. _____

99. _____

100. _____

CASH ADVANCE # 15
BE RELENTLESSLY PERSISTENT

"Success is stumbling from failure to failure with no loss of enthusiasm."

— Winston S. Churchill

When you are in your pursuit to become your best self and maximize your full potential there are going to be times in which you will be met with temporary defeat but it is important to understand that you are not a failure when you fail you are a failure when you give up. Every decision to keep going is a testament to the commitment you have made to your success.

When I first started my journey to become a banker and ultimately reach the C-Suite it would seem as if it was a smooth ride, but the truth is that there were many times that I was passed up for a promotion or many times where I thought that I should've been paid more money and I wasn't. But I was relentless in my pursuit, I was persistent, and I knew that every single day that I kept going after my dream that eventually my dream would come true.

Even as an entrepreneur there are times in which someone doesn't see my vision, or a partner doesn't say yes fast enough or doors get close in my face but the end result being in my mind's eye and me understanding why I do what I do keeps me going

It is imperative that you accomplish something every day. It's definitely not going to be easy, but I promise you it will be worth it. It's always too early to quit so never give up on your hopes and dreams and allow yourself the grace to take a break when you need it but **NEVER** give up! **YOU ARE UNSTOPPABLE!!!!**

CRACKING THE CODE:

Affirmation for persistence

I am persistent in reaching my goals

I press on until the goal is reached.

I achieve everything I set out to do

I am motivated by moving towards my goals

I make my life-choices based on who and what I will become (and am becoming, through these choices).

I am persistent, I never give up. No matter what

I keep going when the going gets tough.

I am Strong, Disciplined, Persistent and Resilient.

I will be persistent in all that I do

I persist and persevere - no matter what.

I have not failed. I've just found ways that won't work

The greater the obstacle the more glory there is in overcoming it

CASH ADVANCE # 16
EXCEED YOUR EXPECTATIONS

"The greatest achievement is to outperform yourself."

- Denis Waitley

Competing against others is one of the worst things that you can do while on your journey and is disrespectful to you and your gift because everybody is unique in their own right. So, as you waste time looking to your left or right, you could be focusing on you and making yourself better. To that end the greatest feeling that you can ever have on earth is to set a goal for yourself and overachieve on that goal. Make sure that you are doing everything in excellence, and you are going the extra mile for you and your dreams. Don't give time and energy towards a job or other people and not focus on giving yourself the same type of love and energy. Make sure you are going above and beyond for your dreams as well as for those who support your mission and vision.

When you go above and beyond what is expected of you, you are sending out a boomerang in which others will go above and beyond for you; so in essence being selfless can be a selfish move to get you more blessings.

Abundance is your birthright so whatever your goals are double or triple them, even quadruple them, know that you can have, be, or do anything you put your mind to. Why not make yourself even prouder than you thought you could? Does this mean set goals so small that you can do them with little to no effort? NO. But stretch yourself beyond your limits and see how far you can go.

CRACKING THE CODE:

Make a list of 20 things you want to do, 20 things you want to have, and 20 things you want to be before you die.

Make sure as you are creating your list; you are not just listing them but making sure they are **S.M.A.R.T**... Meaning...

Specific

Measurable

Achievable

Realistic and

Timely.

It's not enough to say "I want to save more money," but how much do you want to save and why do you want to save it? Is it achievable and realistic for you to save that amount based on your current circumstance? So instead of "I want to save more money," a S.M.A.R.T. goal will say, "I am going to save $5,000 into my Financial Freedom Fund (FFF) by this time next year.

20 Things I Want to Do:

1._____

2._____

3._____

4._____

5._____

6._____

7._____

8._____

9._____

10._____

11._____

12._____

13._____

14._____

15._____

16._____

17._____

18._____

19._____

20._____

20 Things I Want to Have:

1._____

2._____

3._____

4._____

5._____

6._____

7._____

8._____

9._____

10._____

11._____

12._____

13._____

14._____

15._____

16._____

17._____

18._____

19._____

20._____

20 Things I Want to BE:

1._____

2._____

3._____

4._____

5._____

6._____

7._____

8._____

9._____

10._____

11._____

12._____

13._____

14._____

15._____

16._____

17._____

18._____

19._____

20._____

CASH ADVANCE # 17
SURROUND YOURSELF WITH SUCCESSFUL PEOPLE

"You cannot hang out with negative people and expect to live a positive life. ONLY surround yourself with people who are going to lift you higher."

- Oprah Winfrey

Serious Question: Would you rather take relationship advice from your single aunt or from your 2nd cousin who's been married 40 years? Should you take money advice from your broke uncle or from Mr. Johnny who's had a successful business for years and can show you a thing or two about making money? Success leaves clues and for most of us we have an allegiance to our friends and family to provide us with advice and a blueprint to success but most of them have never done or been where we are aiming to go!

Your surroundings play a big part in your success or failure. You may think that on the surface your job, your family, and friends are not influencing your thoughts, but it is what you see every day that makes you who you are.

They say you are the average of the 5 people you spend the most time with, so as you look at your phone and see who were the last 5 people you spoke to, or who you hang out with on a daily basis, ask yourself if these people are adding to your success or taking away from it.

As I started to become more successful, I had to surround myself with people who were on the same mission or greater. It wasn't that I lost love for my day ones, but I had to make a decision to not be the smartest person in the room. I had to level up and be around people who would push me to exceed my limits. Don't get me wrong some of those people are my day ones but everybody couldn't go. Who you surround yourself with and who you love are not mutually exclusive; every relationship has its advantages so make sure you are clear on which ones you will spend your precious time with. I believe **EVERYONE** in a relationship should provide value. It has to be a give and take in order for it to be worthwhile. If a relationship is one sided, then someone is a thief, and the other person is allowing it.

You are 100% responsible for the energy you allow into your space so make sure you are being selective with your circle. Avoid toxic people at all costs and surround yourself with successful people who have a track record of going where you want to go.

CRACKING THE CODE:

The following are ways to attract your success tribe to you:

1. Define Who You Want to Attract to Your Tribe

Make sure you understand the kinds of people you want to attract in your life. What qualities do they have and how can you help each other elevate?

2. Define Who You Need to become in order to attract them

Sometimes it's not about who you know but who knows you! Successful people are not just waiting around wanting to connect with just anybody; they too are looking for certain qualities in their relationships. So, make sure you are accessing who you are and figuring out who you need to become in order to have your tribe seek you out.

3. Increase Your Value

Life is a mirror so if you want to attract a tribe of successful people then become more successful. As you continue to grow and improve yourself, you will begin to attract high-value people into your life. Do things that will increase your personal stock price like read books, travel, get in better shape, attend seminars, get your money right, etc;

4. Put Yourself in The Right Environments

Successful high-value people all frequent the same places. Once your know exactly who your tribe is, ask yourself, "What kinds of environments do my people hang out in?" This may mean attending seminars, golf tournaments, musicals, Broadway plays, cigar lounges, etc; Where they frequent, varies depending on their field of business but do the research then put yourself in that environment.

5. Be of Service

Being of service is the absolute best way to attract your tribe. Instead of trying to ask for something from them off the rip, see how you can serve them. Those who are genuinely ready to serve will be invited into circles with open arms.

CASH ADVANCE # 18
BE TRUTHFUL ABOUT YOUR FLAWS

""When you are completely honest about yourself, there is very little people can say about you that's going to have a negative impact."

-Charlamagne Tha God

Achieving your dreams and aspirations isn't about being perfect, it's about being authentic and being who you say you are. In the words of Dr. Seuss, "Be who you are and say what you feel because those who mind don't matter and those who matter don't mind." This means that you are not trying to hide parts of yourself that are vital to your working relationships. It means that if you need to give a colleague constructive criticism that you won't hesitate to because you understand how important it is to live in your truth. Being truthful about your flaws isn't about complaining or focusing on the negative aspects of yourself, it is about not trying to hide parts of you or sweeping those parts under the rug.

Maximizing your full potential is about living in your truth unapologetically and being 100% comfortable with who you are Today. Made some mistakes in the past? They own up to them! Made some decisions that are not clear? Then get people clear as to why you did what you did. Don't make assumptions about what people understand or what they are willing to tolerate; make sure that you are meeting misunderstandings head on.

CRACKING THE CODE:

AFFIRMATION FOR UNLOCKING YOUR AUTHENTICITY:

1. I am imperfect, and I am okay with that because that makes me interesting and worthy of exploration.

2. I am safe being who I am.

3. My worth isn't something I need to prove; it's just who I am.

4. My worth is immeasurable.

5. I am learning to enjoy the journey of me.

6. I am too busy falling in love with my life to let comparison distract me.

7. Others' opinions are reflections of who they are, so I don't base my self-worth on them.

8. I am always honest and say what's on my mind, unapologetically.

9. I am always treated with, honesty, integrity and respect at all time.

10. I am fair and honest with everyone at all times

CASH ADVANCE # 19
EMBRACE CHANGE

"You never change things by fighting the existing reality. To change something, build a new model that makes the existing model obsolete."

—Buckminster Fuller

It is said that the 3 C's of life are choices, chances and changes... You must make a choice to take a chance, or your life will never change! No matter how our lives may look right now we were not given another opportunity to maximize our full potential just to stay the same... if that were the case our ability to dream and yearn for better would make no sense! The fact that we are given free will to be whatever we want to be is our indication that we must be constantly evolving! Life is for living! Plain and Simple! And if we don't change, we don't grow and If we don't grow, we aren't really living! So, reject anyone and anything that is trying to force you to stay the same! **DO NOT SPARE YOUR CHANGE!!**

Know that change is at the core and essence of happiness! And as Steve Jobs once said... "Here's to the crazy ones. The misfits. The rebels. The troublemakers. The round pegs in the square holes. The ones who see things differently. They're not fond of rules. And they have no respect for the status quo. You can quote them, disagree with them, glorify or vilify them. About the only thing you can't do is ignore them. Because they change things. They push the human race forward. And while some may see them as the crazy ones, we see genius. Because the people who are crazy enough to think they can change the world, are the ones who do."

Embrace change and be crazy enough to change the world. Constantly evolve into a new you on a daily basis because every day is another opportunity to do it better than the day before.

CRACKING THE CODE:

Ask yourself the below questions if you ever become afraid of change:

Why is change happening now?

_____

_____

_____

_____

_____

Why am I afraid of change?

_____

_____

_____

_____

_____

What is the risk of not changing?

_____

_____

_____

_____

_____

_____

_____

What are the benefits of supporting the change?

_____

_____

_____

_____

_____

_____

_____

Reflect on your answers above and see if you can push through your fear to allow change or do you have a valid reason to want things to remain status quo.

CASH ADVANCE # 20
EARN MORE BY INCREASING YOUR KNOWLEDGE

"An investment in knowledge pays the best interest."

-Benjamin Franklin

Financial freedom and living your best life isn't only about the ability to save money but it is about the ability to earn it and make it work for you. The issue that many people run into is that once they reach a certain level of success, they begin to get comfortable and not do what it takes to sustain their position. This is the deadliest of business and finance sin. This sin, the one you must avoid at all costs is called complacency. Complacency as defined by Webster's dictionary is "self-satisfaction especially when accompanied by unawareness of actual dangers or deficiencies". This simply means that someone is satisfied with their level of success and because of this they close a blind eye to the dangers that can possibly change their situation.

Most people remain complacent because they are egotistical about their current position. Most people work so hard to get into successful positions in their life and think that they are the only ones that can ever work that hard. They feel that they are unique and that no one else could fit in their shoes and do what they do. While it is true that they are a unique being, one must realize that harping too much on past successes will lead to loss of status or position because one is not keeping up with change.

Keep your ego in check. Working towards a goal of any sort requires patience, consistency and dedication to said goal. If your goal is big enough, you will have some challenges along the way. Keep going. Become a master. Hone in on your gifts. Devise an impact plan and the income will follow. Never stop learning because the more you know the more you will grow

CRACKING THE CODE:

In the space provided below name some skills that would help you advance in your current business or career then google any books, courses, certificates, or seminars that can help you further develop those skills:

1._____

2._____

3._____

4._____

5._____

6._____

7._____

8._____

9._____

10._____

CASH ADVANCE # 21
BECOME A LEADER WORTH FOLLOWING

"A leader is one who knows the way, goes the way, and shows the way."

- *John Maxwell*

There is an African proverb that says, "If you want to go fast, go alone, but if you want to go further go together." If you want to maximize your full potential and take your life to the next level, then you are going to have to delegate your way to success but ask yourself this… If you were the supervisor on your job (any job), would you want to work for you? Ask yourself this question to do an honest assessment of what you need to improve. Good leaders are good followers, hard workers, they motivate their team(s), competent, fair, honest, dependable, loyal and reliable at a minimum. Do you embody these things? If not, how can you improve?

I was fortunate enough to have some great leaders to emulate during my journey, like Edwin Cintron at Blockbuster and Michael Black at Chase. I also had some not-so-great leaders that I learned from as well because they taught me what not to do. Make sure you are honing in on your leadership skill in order to begin to move in the right direction of your desires.

CRACKING THE CODE:

The following are my favorite leadership books of all time. Make plans to read at least 3 of them this year:

THE 7 HABITS OF HIGHLY EFFECTIVE PEOPLE: POWERFUL LESSONS IN PERSONAL CHANGE BY STEPHEN R. COVEY

The #1 National Bestseller that offers a holistic, integrated, principle-centered approach for solving personal and professional problems. Originally published in 1989, The 7 Habits of Highly Effective People remains consistently relevant even as present-day challenges have become increasingly difficult. Live a life of great and enduring purpose with this business classic

THE 21 IRREFUTABLE LAWS OF LEADERSHIP: FOLLOW THEM AND PEOPLE WILL FOLLOW YOU BY JOHN C. MAXWELL

Maxwell, the world-renowned leadership expert, has authored dozens of books (Leadershift, The 360 Degree Leader, Leadership Gold) dealing with this topic that have sold millions of copies. In The 21 Irrefutable Laws of Leadership, each of the laws has its own chapter that when read, understood, and put into practice, help to guide readers toward setting direction, aligning people, motivating, and inspiring – all with the ultimate goal of creating a leader that people want to follow.

THE ART OF WAR BY SUN TZU

The Art of War is an ancient Chinese military treatise dating back more than 2,000 years ago. The work, which is attributed to the ancient Chinese military strategist Sun Tzu, is composed of 13 chapters – each one is devoted to an aspect of warfare and how it applies to military strategy and tactics. The Art of War is one of the most influential strategy texts in East Asian warfare and has influenced military thinking, business tactics, legal strategy and beyond.

GOOD TO GREAT: WHY SOME COMPANIES MAKE THE LEAP ... AND OTHERS DON'T BY JIM COLLINS

Collins, the bestselling author of Built to Last, and his team of researchers identified 11 elite companies that made the leap from simply "good" to "great" performance. By introducing us to the time-tested business ideas of Level 5 Leaders, The Hedgehog Concept, and A Culture of Discipline, Good to Great offers leaders a complete framework for success. If there exists a must-read business book, this is it.

HOW TO WIN FRIENDS & INFLUENCE PEOPLE BY DALE CARNEGIE

First published in 1936, this classic self-help book has sold more than 15 million copies worldwide. Carnegie's advice about persuasion, career advancement, communication, and influence are as important and relevant today as they were when the book was first published. Achieve your maximum potential with How to Win Friends & Influence People.

THE LEAN STARTUP: HOW TODAY'S ENTREPRENEURS USE CONTINUOUS INNOVATION TO CREATE RADICALLY SUCCESSFUL BUSINESSES BY ERIC RIES

This entrepreneurial masterpiece is a must-read for anyone thinking about going into business for themselves. The Lean Startup introduces a methodology that focuses you on finding out what customers want as quickly as possible and then using scientific experimentation to prove that you're making progress. Ries recommends launching as early and cheaply as possible, so you don't waste time and money getting into the marketplace.

THE ONE MINUTE MANAGER BY
KEN BLANCHARD & SPENCER JOHNSON

For decades, The One Minute Manager has helped millions achieve more successful professional and personal lives. As compelling today as it was when it was originally released more than thirty years ago, this classic parable of a young man looking for an effective manager is as relevant and useful as ever.

PRIMAL LEADERSHIP: UNLEASHING THE POWER
OF EMOTIONAL INTELLIGENCE BY DANIEL
GOLEMAN, RICHARD BOYATZIS & ANNIE MCKEE

The book that established "emotional intelligence" in the business lexicon. Great leaders move us. They ignite our passion and inspire the best in us. When we try to explain why they're so effective, we often speak of strategy, vision, or powerful ideas. But the reality is much more primal – great leadership works through the emotions. Primal Leadership describes what managers and executives must do to become emotionally intelligent leaders. A must-read for anyone that leads or aspires to lead.

START WITH WHY: HOW GREAT LEADERS INSPIRE
EVERYONE TO TAKE ACTION BY SIMON SINEK

From the bestselling author of Leaders Eat Last, Start With Why posits that people won't truly buy into a product, service, movement, or idea until they understand the WHY behind it. Drawing on a wide range of real-life stories, Sinek weaves together a clear vision of what it truly takes to lead and inspire

TRIBES: WE NEED YOU TO LEAD US BY SETH GODIN

While best-selling author Seth Godin has authored more than 15 books (Free Prize Inside, Linchpin, Purple Cow), we consistently refer back to Tribes as our favorite. If you're a leader looking to mobilize an audience (think employees, customers, investors, readers) around a central idea or want them to take a particular course of action, then this Godin book will provide the blueprint for you.

CASH ADVANCE # 22
BUILD A TEAM THAT CAN SUPPORT YOUR VISION

There is no such thing as being self-made. You will reach your goals only with the help of others."

-George Shinn

Who is your tribe? What are their strengths? What are your strengths? What motivates them? What motivates you? When building your team, you will need to consider these things to ensure cohesion. No matter what, make sure you all share a common goal that involves impact and income will follow. How will you and your team add value to your community and eventually the world? Make sure you understand what your team members really want in order for you to be an effective leader and guide them the right way.

When I managed employees as a banker it was the right team members that allowed me to reach all of my goals as a branch manager. There were times when I had to terminate those who weren't moving the ship along but that's part of the game. If you know what motivates people at the outset you won't have to spend too much time trying to get them to do what needs to be done. As an entrepreneur it becomes even more important to find the right people because you have more at stake. The Law of Attraction works for everything so make sure you are clear on who you want to attract and allow your energy to guide you towards the right people.

CRACKING THE CODE:

Below are some sample questions you should ask potential team members:

- What are the first three things you would do in the role?

- If you could change one thing about how we do things in your area, based on what you know, what would it be and why?

- How would you measure success in this role?

- Tell me about the best boss/client that you've ever had. What did you like about them, and why?

- How much oversight/interaction do you like to have from your manager when working on a project?

- How do you like to receive feedback? How do you like to give feedback?

- Do you have experience working on a remote/online team? What do you think the challenges of working remotely are, and how would you handle them?

- If you needed feedback from a remote team member right away but they weren't responsive, what would your next step be?

- If you're a freelancer with multiple clients, tell me about how you balance deadlines and priorities across different teams.

- Tell me about a time that you messed up. How did you fix it?

- Tell me about a time that you had a difficult interaction with a co-worker. How did you resolve it?

- Tell me about a time that you successfully led a project. Who did you work with? What were the challenges? What was the outcome?

- What was the last thing you learned?

- What was the last thing you taught someone?

- When was the last time you totally lost yourself in doing something?

- How do you feel you make a difference in the world?

- Do you have any questions for me?

CASH ADVANCE # 23
LEARN FROM EVERYBODY!

*"When you realize that you can learn something from everyone,
everyone will become someone."*

- Unknown

If you are from any hood then you know that the smartest people are usually the ones that don't look like it. In fact, coming up, my friends and I learned a lot of valuable lessons from the Whinos standing in front of the liquor store. One of my best friends, Quise would always embrace everyone, from young kids to the seniors, executives, gangsters, and drug addicts; He treated everyone the same and his grace towards their knowledge is why he is so well rounded to this day. Watching him taught me a few lessons that I have used to become successful. I know that ANYONE who is in my energy is here to teach me something. I don't judge people, nor do I dismiss anyone regardless of what they may appear to be on the surface. What we need to realize is that EVERYONE is someone and EVERYONE you come in contact with is here to teach you a lesson on your journey. Dismiss them then you are dismissing the message and may have to keep going through the same things until you get it.

Effective immediately I need you to not count someone out because of race, age, gender, background, or anything for that matter. We can all learn from one another even if the lesson is what NOT to do or HOW to be. Learn anyway

CRACKING THE CODE:

Think about all of the people you came across today. Who are they? What did you notice about them? And What lessons could they have been here to teach you? Use the space below to write your answers:

_____

_____

_____

_____

_____

_____

_____

_____

_____

_____

_____

_____

_____

_____

_____

CASH ADVANCE # 24
MASTERMIND YOUR WAY TO SUCCESS

"Deliberately Seek The Company Of People Who Influence You To Think And Act On Building The Life You Desire."

- Napoleon

The concept of the "mastermind alliance" was introduced by Napoleon Hill in the classic book, "Think And Grow Rich," and is the process of combining like minds in order to create a greater force. Hill defines it as "The coordination of knowledge and effort of two or more people, who work toward a definite purpose, in the spirit of harmony." Forming a Mastermind group is imperative in your quest for financial abundance and living your best life.

Each person serves as an accountability partner for one another. They challenge each other to set powerful goals and push each other to accomplish them. Masterminding is about commitment, confidentiality, willingness to give and receive advice and ideas, and the support of one another with total honesty, respect and compassion. Spending time with this person/group will undoubtedly move you closer to ALL of your dreams and aspirations.

My good friend Mike McFadgen aka Cobaine Ivory has been my Mastermind partner for close to a decade and I can honestly say that the way we held each other accountable for our goals has helped tremendously as we both took strides in our respective fields. I've also been a part of other mastermind groups like "Meeting of the Business Minds" led by my brother Taqiy or The Elevate Money Mastermind that included all the top Black Financial Minds on the planet. Each has held me accountable in ways that I am forever grateful for. I've even created my own mastermind programs like Mailbox Money Academy and the Abundance Community that has produced many five and six figure entrepreneurs. So far, we had one seven-figure earner.

Who do you brainstorm with? Who do you share your ideas with and how do you prepare to get things done? If you have a bunch of great ideas and never execute them, you will invest a lot of time and have no return. You always want to have a return on investment (ROI) which is where you invest something (for example time/money) and get back what you invested (or more) from taking those steps. Plan, believe and act in success. A mastermind group will help you get it done.

CRACKING THE CODE:

ACTION: Below make a list of the characteristics you would like in an accountability partner. Begin to identify those who fit the description. If you do not currently know someone that fits, begin putting yourself out there to meet this person. Start a weekly mastermind call or meeting in person if possible. Also join our private Facebook group at https://www.facebook.com/groups/MRUMastermind

_____

_____

_____

CASH ADVANCE # 25
TODAY IS THE ONLY DAY THAT MATTERS

"Your life requires your mindful presence in order to live it. Be here now."

— *Akiroq Brost*

If your aim is to live your absolute best life then you **MUST** stay present! You **MUST** be here and now! You **MUST** realize that this moment is the only moment that matters! All that exists is **RIGHT NOW**. The past has already happened and regardless of who you know or how much money you have there is no way you can bring back the past and the future is yet to come and truth be told it will **NEVER** come because even if tomorrow arrives, we can **ONLY** experience it **TODAY**!

So many of us are disrespecting today and worrying about a tomorrow that isn't even guaranteed. Take one second, minute, hour and day at a time. Each of these are a gift and it is the only currency that we have for sure.

In the past, anytime I would feel depressed it was because I was looking too far back and whenever I felt anxious it was because I was looking too far in the future. The moment I started to realize that the only thing I had any control over was the present moment was the moment I started to live in peace.

Each and every moment presents you with a point of choice. You can choose love and enjoy now, or you can choose fear and worry about a time that doesn't even exist. I choose love every single time! Be Here and Now and know that everything is perfect, and you are **EXACTLY** where you are supposed to be.

CRACKING THE CODE:

AFFIRMATIONS TO BE MORE PRESENT:

I am here right now. All that exists is now.

I am in the perfect place at the perfect time.

My point of power is in the present moment.

I allow myself to feel my feelings no matter what they are.

The Universe ONLY speaks to me in the present moment.

I do the best I can, with the resources that I have, I am grateful.

CASH ADVANCE # 26
GET COMFORTABLE WITH THE UNCOMFORTABLE TRUTH

"When you are able to maintain your own highest standards of integrity – regardless of what others may do or think – you are destined for greatness."

-Napoleon Hill

Bad news doesn't get better with time. Be honest. Be up front. Have tact, but express yourself. People will respect you more because of your honesty even if the news is bad. For many years I was a people pleaser. I cared about how people felt so I would lie, omit the truth, and let people down easy just so that I could lessen the blow of the truth. When I did that I only made things worse and prolonged an unwanted situation. I never came out better by doing this in fact, I jeopardized a lot of important relationships trying to appease people.

My best friend, life partner, and wife Amina was the opposite. She told the truth fast with clarity and made sure there were never any misunderstandings. I began to adopt this in my life, and it did wonders for my relationships. I gained a greater level of respect from my peers and those who I was delivering the truth to, appreciated that I wasn't wasting their time.

Make sure you get comfortable with the uncomfortable truth. Telling lies or omitting the truth is a self-made prison and like the scripture says… The Truth shall set you free!

CRACKING THE CODE:

In the space below, write down a few times that you didn't tell someone the truth because of how you thought it would make them feel. Were you justified? Did it make the situation better or worse? How could you have told them the truth without being mean or malicious?

_____

_____

_____

_____

_____

_____

_____

_____

_____

_____

_____

_____

_____

CASH ADVANCE # 27
BECOME A MASTER OF YOUR WORDS

"Be Impeccable with Your Word
Speak with integrity. Say only what you mean. Avoid using the word
to speak against yourself or to gossip about others. Use the power of
your word in the direction of truth and love."

-Don Miguel Ruiz

B y now you should know a few things about the Law of Attraction; You should know that your thoughts become things, that what you resist will persist, and that you will always get what you focus on. One of the most overlooked portions of the Law of Attraction is that you get what you put out there or you reap what you sow. Life is a boomerang so as you do unto others you are actually doing unto you. This is why it is imperative that you become a master of your words.

In the classic book, *The Four Agreements* by Don Miguel Ruiz he gives the first agreement which is to Be Impeccable with Your Word. He describes this as speaking with integrity, honesty, and truthfulness; saying only what you mean; speaking of what you desire and avoiding speaking negatively about yourself or others. In other words, **ONLY** use your words in the positive direction of truth and love. Ruiz explains that your words are magic. He says that you can use your words to create good in the world, or to create chaos and spread negativity.

This is important to take heed to from so many levels. When you speak ONLY good of yourself and others, ONLY good will be your experience. Also, when you have a reputation of speaking impeccably of others regardless of who it is, it allows other people to trust you more which increases your level of respect. As our mothers use to say to us: If you don't have anything good to say then don't say anything at all. Become a master of your words and continue to live your life to the fullest>

CRACKING THE CODE:

HERE ARE 3 WAYS YOU CAN BE IMPECCABLE WITH YOUR WORD:

1. ONLY focus on the Positive Aspects of Your Current Circumstances

Shift your words to more positive statements from where you are. You can shift from "I'm tired of being broke" to "I'm excited for the opportunity to build wealth." You can shift from "I'm so busy" to "I'm so thankful to have so many opportunities to maximize my full potential." Even though they are small shifts, they can make you feel better and the energy in the sentence will begin to attract the experiences that you desire.

2. Instead of speaking of the problem, start using your words to speak of the solution.

Instead of focusing on what you don't have or what's gone wrong, think about the solution you hope for and all the ways things could go right in the future.

3. Don't Speak Ill of ANYONE

Make sure you are not participating in gossip and/or delighting in the downfall of anyone. What you want for your brother or sister you should want for yourself so make sure you are wishing **EVERYONE** well.

CASH ADVANCE # 28
APPRECIATE EVERYTHING!

"You will never get what you want until you are thankful for what you have"

-Michael P. Watson

Gratitude is the most powerful way to create a mindset shift and attract more abundance into your life. Take a minute and close your eyes. Put your hand on your heart and begin to appreciate everything and everyone you are grateful for. This includes the less favorable things that at first seemed "bad" or "negative" but now you realize they have taught you invaluable life lessons. Be grateful for it all because the experience is what has shaped you to be who you are today and what will continue to help shape who you become tomorrow.

As Eckhart Tolle once said, "Acknowledging the good that you already have in your life is the foundation for all abundance." As you reflect, I want you to take a deep breath in and out and appreciate the air that you breathe. Realize that 150,000 people die each day but you were given another opportunity to maximize your full potential. Give thanks that you still have purpose and appreciate all of your abundance that is here now and of those that will surely come.

Keep an attitude of gratitude for all things. The more thankful you are, the more you will have to be thankful for.

CRACKING THE CODE:

ACTION: In the space below make a list of the things that you are grateful for. Write them in the affirmative beginning with I AM grateful for…. After you write them down, stand up and repeat them aloud.

_____

_____

_____

_____

_____

_____

_____

_____

_____

_____

_____

_____

_____

_____

CASH ADVANCE # 29
PUT MONEY IN ITS PLACE

"Don't be too impressed by the allure of money. Money is just a by-product of helping people with your gift. Focus on the mission, not the money."

-Steve Harvey

Many people believe that in order to live their best lives they must chase after money, but the truth is that money is merely a tool. Money makes a great servant but it's a terrible master. Because many of us give money so much power we give up the real power we have to live a financially abundant life. Money has never been and will **NEVER** be your source. You have **EVERYTHING** you need already to live the life of your dreams.

If you chase money, then it will merely run from you and elude you. What you need to realize is that money has a thing for value. The more value you provide the more money you will have.

Instead of working hard for money, money needs to work hard for you.

Whether you come from money or not it is imperative that you begin to give **VALUE** in order to accumulate funds. The first step is to start with active income, but eventually, you need that relationship to switch and allow passive income to be your best friend.

What's the difference between active income and passive income?

Active income is when you trade time for money. For example, if you work a 9 to 5 job, you are investing a considerable amount of time in exchange for a paycheck every week, bi-weekly, bi-monthly, or monthly. If you stop working, you don't get paid. So, in essence, your time equals money.

Passive income, on the other hand, is getting money without having to trade your time. You may have to put in a lot of time during the initial setup, but after that time is invested, money keeps flowing even while you sleep.

For example, you invest in stock and that stock pays you a dividend quarterly without you doing much, you rent out an apartment you own and receive monthly income without lifting a finger, or you write a book, and that book pays you royalties each month.

In this case, you invest your time only during the initial set up. The product or service you developed during that time starts earning money for you over a period of time (mostly in perpetuity) without you investing much time further.

Begin today creating a plan for creating passive income in order to put money in its rightful place

CRACKING THE CODE:

The following is how to diversify your income and create multiple streams:

1. Work to learn + Earn

We talked about this earlier but here's a recap: most people get a job to earn money, but that is the worst use of time if that's all you're getting. To build multiple streams of income, you have to make sure that while you are working, you are also learning a skill that is transferable as an entrepreneur. Make sure that whatever you are doing to earn money increases your value and teaches you lessons that you can monetize off of later.

2. Use knowledge to solve a problem

With your newfound knowledge, it is time to use it to solve a problem. In fact, a problem solver is the definition of an entrepreneur; someone who gets paid to solve a problem. Whether you do this full-time or on the side, understand that your knowledge is valuable and that's what's going to begin the process of earning you an income independent of your 9-5 or contract work.

3. Use Money to Make Money

Now that you have started to accumulate money, instead of using that money to buy things, use that money to purchase income-producing assets. These income-producing assets are going to be your multiple streams of income.

4. REPEAT!!!!!!

Now it's time to repeat the process.

1. Work to learn and earn

2. Use your knowledge to solve a problem

3. Use the money you make from solving your problem to make more money by investing in another income-producing asset.

Repeating this process will give you everything you need to create financial freedom.

Below are the Common Types of (Passive) Streams of Income check the list and aim to create at least 4 streams of income:

1. Interest – from a variety of loans, either to individuals (peer to peer lending or private notes) or companies (bonds, notes)

2. Dividends – from investments, partnerships

3. Capital gains – from the sale of investments

4. Royalties – from products you sell or license

5. Rental income – from real estate

6. Business income – which may or may not be passive, but the idea is you build something that generates income without active work, like a website or the sale of information products

CASH ADVANCE # 30
DON'T TAKE ANYTHING
PERSONALLY

"Nothing others do is because of you. What others say and do is a projection of their own reality, their own dream. When you are immune to the opinions and actions of others, you won't be the victim of needless suffering."

-Don Miguel Ruiz

W hen I tell you this advice is sooooooo clutch!!! It will change your whole entire life and give you the peace and prosperity that you deserve. Especially as someone who came from the hood, we were taught that respect comes before **EVERYTHING,** so we took everything personal just in case someone was trying to disrespect us we needed to put it check fast. As someone who understands the streets on every level, I know why this is an important survival mechanism and vital to your well-being... **BUT**... What got you here will not get you there. Taking everything personal is a defense mechanism that attracts energy to you that will **NOT** allow you to maximize your full potential. That's why it's important to adopt Mr. Don Miguel Ruiz's second agreement... **DON'T TAKE ANYTHING PERSONALLY**

To restate his quote from the book, "Whatever happens around you, don't take it personally. Nothing other people do is because of you. It is because of themselves. All people live in their own dream, in their own mind; they are in a completely different world from the one we live in. When we take something personally, we make the assumption that they know what is in our world, and we try to impose our world on their world."

This is so profound because it is a fact that everyone has their own unique experiences, and it is those experiences that people use to create their perspective on life. No two people have the same perspectives, so our actions, thoughts, and words are a reflection of our unique perspective and experiences so even when it seems like we are talking about someone else we are really projecting our own perspective and experiences.

For example, I grew up with people telling me I wasn't worth much so in order to get people's attention I would act up to prove my worth. When I got into corporate America, I created this same story that because I was young, black, or fill in the blank _____, I had to work hard to "prove my worth." As I transition to entrepreneurship, this perspective lingered, so anytime someone didn't give me my proper just due I would get offended and automatically believe that they were "hating on me" or "Intimidated by my greatness" not realizing that their perspective was totally different and hate or intimidation wasn't even in their thought process. In fact, in a particular situation in which I confronted someone with my ridiculous claim, I learned that it was actually the opposite, they respected my work so much that they felt that it would be insulting to me to keep trying to give me praise. They literally said, "I know you hear it all the time, so I don't want to seem ingenuine." I realized that taking things personally or frankly trying to feed my ego based on past traumas and experiences was costing me valuable relationships.

So next time you feel snubbed, know that **IT'S NOT ABOUT YOU!** That Facebook or IG post... **IT'S NOT ABOUT YOU!** Even if someone says something to you directly… **IT'S NOT ABOUT YOU!** Repeat After me: What other people think or say about me is **NONE OF MY BUSINESS!!!**

CRACKING THE CODE:

HOW TO NOT TAKE THINGS PERSONAL

I know this won't happen overnight, but it is imperative that you start taking steps to release yourself from the control of other people's thoughts and actions. What other people say or do should not be able to disrupt your peace. Peace comes from within so it's time to tap into it fully.

1. Fall in Love with YOURSELF

When you dedicate time to your self-love and self-acceptance practices you no longer need outside validation in order to feel whole. In fact, when you love yourself fully and hold yourself in the highest regard, that energy allows you to attract others who are similarly comfortable in their own skin so unnecessary friction ceases to exist.

2. Identify Your Emotional Triggers

If you have an emotional reaction to something a person says or does (or your perception of them), it is extremely helpful to name that feeling and notice how it feels in your body. Why does this trigger you? What is the root cause of this perception? Identifying it is the beginning process of healing.

3. Ask for Clarity

Instead of jumping into conclusion and taking your experience and perspective as the filter to judge what someone says or does, ask for clarity. Sometimes understanding what people really mean or where they are really coming from will clear up all discrepancies.

4. Put Your Expectations in Check

Most of us don't realize that we put expectations and entitlements on our relationships and when those expectations aren't met, we take it personally. Next time you feel a way about what someone says or does, check in on your expectations. When you make assumptions about how someone "should act" then you are setting yourself up for disappointment.

5. Share How You are Feeling

We are all human (Or spirits having a human experience) so it's natural that we may fall back into our norm and take things personally. In this case be honest, especially if it's a relationship you care about. Don't hold in your thoughts or feelings and don't just try to sweep them under the rug. If what someone says or does to you makes you feel a kind of way, let them know. Share your feelings and allow that person to understand the impact of their actions (whether real or perceived)

CASH ADVANCE # 31
REMEMBER YOUR WHY AND STAY MOTIVATED

"Life is never made unbearable by circumstances, but only by lack of meaning and purpose."

-Viktor Frankl

If you keep your purpose in your mind's eye then when things get seemingly tough you will be given the motivation to keep going. I'm not trying to guilt you (or maybe I am) but when you REALLY start living out your purpose you will realize that your gift is BIGGER than you. You will realize that YOU are the only person that can fulfil YOUR assignment so there are people who are literally counting on you to show up every single day. Imagine if a heart surgeon had an off day? Well, you are a heart surgeon for someone who needs your gift.

When I first started my financial educator journey, I simply looked at my assignment as a way to make ends meet but gradually as I started to see the impact that I was having on people's family's and on how people changed their whole lives, I started to know that my work was bigger than me. When I get messages from people locked up in prison telling me that my words helped change their life and when they come home, they are going to do things differently or when someone tells me that my work has stopped them from committing suicide or that I helped them become the first business owner in their family; I don't take that responsibility lightly and nor should you.

Know and understand that you matter, and your work is impactful! People are counting on you to show up and share your gift. Remember your Why and Stay Motivated!

CRACKING THE CODE:

AFFIRMATIONS TO KEEP YOU ON PURPOSE

1. I am an unstoppable force of nature.

2. I am a living, breathing example of motivation.

3. I know my assignment and I show up EVERYDAY.

4. I am having a positive and inspiring impact on the people I come into contact with.

5. I am inspiring people through my work.

6. I am filled with focus.

7. I do not waste away a single day of my life. I squeeze every ounce of value out of each of my days on this planet—today, tomorrow, and every day.

8. I finish what matters and let go of what does not.

9. My life has meaning. What I do has meaning. My actions are meaningful and inspiring.

10. When I show up, I change lives! I AM CHANGING LIVES EVERYDAY!

CASH ADVANCE # 32
CREATE YOUR LEGACY NOW

"Carve your name on hearts, not tombstones. A legacy is etched into the minds of others and the stories they share about you."

-Shannon Adler

We all have an expiration date and when it's all said and done no one will remember the size of your house or the kind of car you drove. They won't brag about your bank account or how many countries you were able to visit. They are not going to rejoice about how many followers you had or whether or not you were verified with a blue check; they are simply going to remember the hearts you touched, the people you helped, and the impact you had on the world.

Maximizing your full potential is about living out your life in a way that is making anyone who comes in contact with you better. We must realize that our legacy isn't built once we die, it is built piece by piece every single day. When it's all said and done, maybe the whole world will remember you or maybe just a couple of people, but if you live the right way your name will live on forever.

Create your legacy now! Make every breath you take and every deed you do matter. Write your story and become a living legend.

Also, remember that once upon a time it was illegal for us to document our journey so as you are building your legacy make sure you are documenting the process and showing the world that you are Greatness On Display.

CRACKING THE CODE:

ACTION: WRITE YOUR LIFE STORY

Buy a composition book and begin from the date you were born. Outline each year that something significant happened in your life up until today's date. Next to each significant date, write a brief summary of what happened. Now find someone you trust or hire someone to interview you based on those dates you outlined. Transcribe the interview then edit it and add anything you are missing. After your story is written, keep it in a safe place and write its location in your will so your family members can find it when needed. Going forward use and write a daily journal to keep your story fresh and update you book every 5-10 years

CASH ADVANCE # 33
STOP PLAYING SMALL AND BE THE GIANT THAT YOU ARE

"You are a child of God. Your playing small does not serve the world. There is nothing enlightened about shrinking so that other people won't feel insecure around you. We are all meant to shine, as children do. We were born to make manifest the glory of God that is within us. It's not just in some of us; it's in everyone. And as we let our own light shine, we unconsciously give other people permission to do the same."

-Marianne Williamson

G rowing up in the hood and getting to a position in which you are elevating your life, you are going to undoubtedly meet with people who are not necessarily pleased with your success. As we stated before; don't take it personally because it has **NOTHING** to do with you. You are shattering their limiting beliefs and in order for them to be ok with being average they have to justify their excuses.

This is not to put any negative energy in the air, but please be aware that these same people will try to dim your light. They will tell you to be humble and act as if you being confident in **YOURSELF** is an atrocious act. Make sure that while on your journey you are not turning down your light in order to fit in or to make anyone comfortable.

The fact of the matter is that there is a big difference between being arrogant, conceited, self-centered or confident. Arrogance and conceit are about using what you have to put others down and make others feel inferior. Being self-centered is about caring only about you and not using your gifts to bring others up. Confidence on the other hand is about taking pride in who you are and what you've accomplished. It's about the willingness to help others benefit from your experiences because you are confident in your abilities, and you don't worry about competition.

In fact, a confident person knows that the only true competitor that exists in this physical world is the one that lives within. To that end, we need to stop making excuses as to why we are not maximizing our full potential. No matter how hard you try you will never be able to please everyone! There are going to be many people who do not like you simply because of your confidence.

Oh the (Insert Expletive) Well! You were put here to be the best that you can be and those who belittle your ambition do not deserve to be part of your circle. Only a Knife can sharpen a Knife so make sure you are surrounding yourself with people who will take you higher! Let your light shine. Don't decrease your value to make people feel comfortable. You were born to be great so **LET YOUR GREATNESS** shine!

CRACKING THE CODE:

Revisit your "Top 100 Win list" from Cash Advance #14 and remind yourself how much you are the Ish! Now below in the space provided; Write the top 20 things you **WILL** accomplish in the near future but write them using "I am" for example: I am The Greatest Money Mindset Coach on the Planet!

1._____

2._____

3._____

4._____

5._____

6._____

7._____

8._____

9._____

10._____

11._____

12._____

13._____

14._____

15._____

16._____

17._____

18._____

19._____

20._____

CASH ADVANCE # 34
CHANGE YOUR PERSPECTIVE ON STRUGGLE

If there is no struggle, there is no progress.

- Frederick Douglass

They say life is not easy for those who dream. Those who have great aspirations will often be met with many setbacks and temporary defeat. On the other hand, those who want to remain mediocre or stay oblivious to what life has to offer will be satisfied with just getting by. Despite the disparity it is absolutely unacceptable to not maximize your full potential!

The struggles you deal with in life are in no way supposed to cripple you. They are here to make you stronger and remove every ounce of doubt and weakness you have in your body. You are more powerful than you even know and nothing in this world can stop you unless you allow it.

Embrace your struggles and **NEVER** allow circumstances to dictate what you can or can't accomplish. Life is abundant and anything you want out of it will be yours if you absolutely believe that you can have it. Your setbacks are a setup for your comeback. Your life is like a bow and arrow; before the arrow can fully realize its power, the bow must first be taken back as far as it can. But once it reaches the point of no return and it is let go; God help anything that is in its path! **BE THE ARROW!** Understand that no matter how far you are taken back you **CANNOT AND WILL NOT LOSE** because the force that is behind you can break through anything.

Embrace the struggle and dream as far as you can dream and believe in your power to make those dreams come true. As Henry Ford once said, "There are those who think they can and those who think they can't" Be the former and live life to the fullest!

CRACKING THE CODE:

AFFIRMATION TO PUT STRUGGLE IN ITS PLACE:

1. I Embrace Struggle! Everything that is happening in my life is making me stronger!

2. There are no problems, only challenges.

3. I welcome challenges into my life.

4. Challenges are opportunities to learn and grow.

5. I can face every obstacle that crosses my path.

6. I'm not going to quit.

7. Tomorrow is a brand-new day.

8. I'm going to face everything that life puts in my way.

9. I can and will survive anything life throws at me.

10. I have the strength and courage to get through any situation.

11. There are no problems, just obstacles I can overcome.

12. I attract positive energy wherever I go.

13. I can solve any challenge.

14. Failure is just another step for success.

15. I know when to persevere along a path and when to let go and change course.

CASH ADVANCE # 35
RELAX OR RESIST (PEACE IS A CHOICE)

"Peace, it does not mean to be in a place where there is no noise, trouble, or hard work. It means to be in the midst of all those things and still be calm in your heart. Peace comes from within. Do not seek it without"

– Buddha

I used to be a big worrier and it absolutely felt horrible. I would be anxious or fearful about an event that probably never happened, but the possibility would keep me up at night. It wasn't until I realized that all I could do, is all I could do, is when I began to let worry go!

If you are in a situation that you can fix... then Fix it!! If you can't fix it... then don't worry because... you can't fix it!! These concepts seem very elementary and simple but despite that a lot of us continue to go against this wisdom day in and day out!

Worry is a disease that is caused by lack of faith! Those who don't believe in the miracles that life has to offer, go around anxious, stressed, and worried, instead of using what is in their control to make the situation better! Our aim should be to live in Peace! And Peace is a choice! We can choose to relax and let things be or we can resist and live in hell on earth.

Effective immediately, I need you to Stop Worrying and Start Living! **ALL YOU CAN DO IS ALL YOU CAN DO!!!!** Stop making your today more complex based on a skewed tomorrow that might not ever get here! Today is the only coin you have... **SPEND IT WISELY!** And in the words of the honorable Bobby McFarlin... **DON'T WORRY... BE HAPPY!!!**

CRACKING THE CODE:

HERE ARE SOME AFFIRMATIONS TO LET GO OF WORRY:

1. I let go of what I can't change and do my best with what I can.

2. I release myself from stress.

3. I find joy in the little things

4. I find joy in where I am.

5. I release worry and know that this too, shall pass.

6. I am safe and in control.

7. I will not stress over things I cannot control.

8. I appreciate my life and find things to be grateful for.

9. I have been through hard things before and have survived them.

10. I have the ability to overcome anxiety.

11. I am worthy of good things.

12. All of my feelings are valid.

13. Everything that is happening now is truly for my highest good.

14. I believe in my ability to get through tough times.

15. I have everything I need within me.

CASH ADVANCE # 36
KNOW THAT YOU ARE MORE THAN ENOUGH

"You alone are enough. You have nothing to prove to anybody."

-Maya Angelou

In full transparency I used to think that in order for me to be loved I had to prove myself worthy. I attached my worthiness to my job title, to the amount of money I had, to my social status. It wasn't until I realized that the uniqueness of having breath in my body is what made me worthy. The fact that God gave me another opportunity to live my best life means that I had still had purpose, so why would I need validation from others when I have already been validated by the Most High.

We know that hurt people sometimes hurt people so my sense of unworthiness has a deeper root but as I started to realize that it didn't matter what I did in the past or what I could do in the future, it was the fact that I was here today that made me more than enough, then I stop allowing people to take advantage of me.

You are already pre-wired with everything you need to be successful. If you are made in the image and likeness of God, how can you not be more than enough. Abundance is Your Birthright so once you understand that fact then you will accept that your mere existence is a gift from God.

CRACKING THE CODE:

The following affirmations are to be read anytime you need a boost of worthiness:

1. I am a special person. There's nobody else like me.

2. I love myself.

3. I love myself more and more each day.

4. I am worthy of love.

5. I am worthy of happiness.

6. I am worthy of success.

7. I deserve to be paid well for my skills.

8. People value my work, my time, and my love.

9. I believe in myself.

10. Nothing can stop me from achieving my dreams.

11. People want to hear my thoughts and opinions. My voice is important.

12. I am perfect just the way I am.

13. I respect myself, and others appreciate me.

14. I am whole and complete.

15. There's nothing I need to do or be to earn love or respect.

16. Everything is possible for me.

17. I have everything I need to succeed.

18. What I want is coming to me.

19. I am worthy of the compliments I receive.

20. My contributions are valued and appreciated.

CASH ADVANCE # 37
DO WHATEVER YOU FEEL (AS LONG AS IT FEELS GOOD)

"Feeling Good leads You To Everything That You Want."

-Abraham Hicks

I consider myself a big kid at heart. I have a hard rule that says, "If I'm not having fun then I no longer want to do it." This includes everything from work to relationships to extracurricular activities. I just believe that life is too short to live in doom and gloom or to do things that you don't want to do. Little did I know that this way of living reality was a cheat code to living your best life and attracting opportunities that bring you closer to your desires. This was made even more clear when I was introduced to a book called *Ask and it is Given* by Esther and Jerry Hicks.

In the book, they thoroughly explain how to activate the laws of the universe to manifest your every desire. In the book there is constant mention of "being in the vortex," which is the equivalent to what we know as "Good vibes," but it is more than just a hashtag or a saying, it is a necessity if you want to live a life of financial freedom, peace, love, and happiness. What is the vortex? It is a term that means alignment to Source energy, the Universe, God, All that is, Allah, Buddha, or whatever you call your higher power. Being in the vortex means that you are one with who you really are, you are tapped into your Godself, you are feeling the best that you can feel and are in vibrational alignment with your desires. When you're in the vortex you are enthusiastic, inspired, passionate and feel joy and appreciation. When you are out of the vortex (or vibrationally unaligned with your source) you feel down, frustrated, hopeless, fearful, and angry. These are the vibes that close the door to your desires and not only block you from living your best life but also cause many unwanted thoughts and feelings. Left unchecked it can really begin to spiral out of control and cause destruction, not only in the mind but in the physical as well.

Knowing this, it is imperative that you focus on feeling good! The feeling that you feel will attract more of those feelings to you and ultimately give you your desires. In my experience, anything that "I had to do" wound up not working out if I did it with an energy that wasn't one of joy. Most of the things that will work out in your life are the things you do with love. That's why most self-help gurus will tell you to do what you love and love what you do. This is because the radiation of love towards your work will bring upon more work that is enjoyable and allows you to live in bliss.

Stop forcing yourself to do work because you feel obligated to. In the end most of it will not work out. Allow yourself to fall in love with your why and **BE THAT** every single day. Fall in love with what you are doing, and only do it when you feel good.

CRACKING THE CODE:

I know only doing what feels good is easier said than done. In fact I know there's someone reading this with the side eye saying that this is contrary to everything they've ever been taught about perseverance and pushing ahead despite how they feel but hear me out for a second.

One of the most intriguing things that I found about *Ask and it is Given* is that it talks about an emotional scale in which you can use to guide you back into the vortex if you are feeling down. The scale goes from 1-22 and the goal is to reach the ultimate high of 1 which is Joy / Knowledge / Empowerment / Freedom / Love / Appreciation. The good thing about this list is that while the goal is to be in the vortex, there is an understanding that life happens and sometimes it can be difficult to be in total alignment at all times, so instead of always aiming for 1 immediately, you start to aim for a better feeling in order to eventually get back to alignment with source energy. Use this list below whenever you are feeling less than yourself and aim to go to the next best feeling.

1. Joy/Knowledge/ Empowerment/ Freedom/Love/Appreciation	12. Disappointment
2. Passion	13. Doubt
3. Enthusiasm/Eagerness/ Happiness	14. Worry
4. Positive Expectation/Belief	15. Blame
5. Optimism	16. Discouragement
6. Hopefulness	17. Anger
7. Contentment	18. Revenge
8. Boredom	19. Hatred/Rage
9. Pessimism	20. Jealousy
10. Frustration/Irritation/ Impatience	21. Insecurity/Guilt/ Unworthiness
11. "Overwhelming"	22. Fear/Grief/Depression/ Despair/Powerlessness

I found this list helpful anytime I was unaligned with my source, I used it to see where I was on the emotional scale and wherever I landed, my goal was to move up the scale, so I can feel better. Thank you, Universe, for this list!

CASH ADVANCE # 38
DON'T BE AFRAID TO TRY
UNCONVENTIONAL APPROACHES

*"No matter where you are in your journey, never forget that what got
you to where you are won't get you to the next level."*

-John C. Maxwell

There's a saying that goes "If it ain't broke, don't fix it." Well, in this case, if something isn't broken but it's not helping you reach your goals, then it **MUST BE FIXED ASAP**! Don't be afraid to reinvent yourself, switch things up or even get help. When I started my journey as an entrepreneur, I learned how to do everything, to be a jack of all trades and get things done. But as I grew, I needed to adjust my thinking and how I approach things in order to get them to the next level. What it took to be a successful employee was not the same things that I needed to be a successful entrepreneur. Sometimes it may seem that there is a logical step that needs to be taken in order to get to the next level but most times it is the unconventional approaches that allow us to make a quantum Leap and exceed our expectations.

Just because you made four figures this year doesn't mean you can't jump to seven. Just because something has never happened in your life doesn't mean that it isn't possible and that you have to live your life in chronological order. Taking unconventional approaches allows you to skip the line because in true Law of Attraction fashion, you get what you focus on and you get what you believe you can have. Think Bigger and allow Exponential Growth!

CRACKING THE CODE:

One of the most powerful books I've ever read is called *You Squared by Price Pritchett*. The book is just 36 pages long, but it's packed with practical insight and actionable takeaways that teach you how to take a quantum leap in your business and life and experience exponential growth in real time.

Pritchett states "we don't have to be content with incremental, gradual change through the application of hard work. Rather, we are capable of an explosive jump in performance at an accelerated rate, and it requires less effort." How you may ask?

Here is a summary:

Quit Trying Harder – Trying harder only produces incremental gains. A quantum shift is an elegant solution requiring less effort.

Ignore Conventional Approaches – A quantum leap requires an abrupt change in behavior. It requires finesse over effort, simplicity over complexity, a new paradigm and a fresh perspective.

Think Beyond What Common Sense Would Allow – Quantum leaps require "uncommon sense." Rethink your thinking. Violate the boundaries of the probable.

Suspend Disbelief – Act as if your success is for certain and proceed boldly.

Focus On Ends Rather Than Means – It is crucial to have a clear picture of what you want to accomplish. Solutions will appear. Draw the map as you go.

Rely On Unseen Forces – When you focus on the clear picture of what you want to accomplish and move confidently toward it, unexpected and unknown resources materialize.

Choose A Different Set Of Rules – You can never avoid risk, you can only choose which risks you will take. Risk believing in yourself.

Trust In The Power Of The Pursuit – Dreams begin to crystallize into reality when they are pursued because the world behaves differently when you go after what you want.

Seek Failure – Unless you are willing to fail, you will never have the opportunity to test the limits of what you are capable of accomplishing.

Get Uncomfortable – Quantum leaps jerk you out of your comfort zone. If you aren't experiencing discomfort, the risk you are taking probably isn't worthy of you.

Open Your Gifts – There are unused gifts waiting to play a role in your quantum leap, open them.

Fall In Love – Create a dramatic dream that goes beyond the 'reasonable', and then allow it to become your "magnificent obsession."

Make Your Move Before You Are Ready – You don't prepare for a quantum leap, you make it… and then you fine-tune as you go.

Look Inside For The Opportunity – Everything else that's needed comes from *inside* you, not from anything outside you.

CASH ADVANCE # 39
LET GO OF EVERYTHING YOU THINK YOU CANNOT LIVE WITHOUT

"Detach from needing to have things work out a certain way. The universe is perfect and there are no failures. Give yourself the gift of detaching from your worries and trust that everything is happening perfectly."

- Unknown

As mentioned in my story, 2019 was a tough year for me. Everything was tested and I felt that my life no longer had meaning. With many of us still recovering from childhood traumas, this is a dangerous place to be in. Many of us often attach ourselves to people, places, and circumstances and believe that those things make us who we are. We expect these things to always be there for us, in the way that we are accustomed to and we use these things as a source of our happiness. The important truth is that **ANYTHING** that you believe you cannot live without is your master and is truly in control of your life. You can **NEVER** have true success or happiness if it is attached to something that can change. The **ONLY** genuine source of security, joy, and happiness is living as your true self. Do not ascribe your identity to your title, your bank account, your popularity, your followers, whether you are loved or hated; not your accolades or accomplishments, not your social status or political affiliations, not your VIP access, the size of your house, or the car you drive. It cannot be attached to your significant other, your kids, siblings, parents, or friends. True happiness comes from within, and as you understand that the Most High God has put you here for a purpose, you will understand that God knows best, so any change in status, connection, or circumstance is part of the master plan.

When you are attached to anything, you begin to feel a sense of anxiety, fear, anger, jealousy, hopelessness, sadness, disconnection, pride, or vanity. This can happen on the inside, even if your outside world seems to be going well. This is why we **MUST** detach ourselves from everything that we think we need. This doesn't mean not love deeply, and it doesn't mean expecting the worst of every situation; it means staying in the moment. Live here and now and take things as they come. Always stay present and enjoy what the present moment brings without creating scenarios that can alter your peace. Live in Peace **NOW!** Accept your blessings **NOW!** And remember that as long as you have breath in your body... **YOU STILL HAVE A PURPOSE!**

CRACKING THE CODE:

PRACTICE THE LAW OF CONSCIOUS DETACHMENT

The Law of Conscious Detachment says that when we accept what is, we accept the unalterable realities in our life without resisting them. This means that you should allow any unpleasant experience in your life that you cannot change to flow through you without resisting it and without allowing it to affect your state of being. By doing this, your ability to live the life you deserve becomes a reality. This concept is not about just letting go but about trusting and believing that everything is working for your good. It is about allowing yourself to focus your energies on the things you can change to create your bliss, which is the state of being that we want to be in, to attract the favorable circumstances that will allow our dreams to come to fruition.

Some things are what they are, and no matter how much we resist them, nothing can be done about them. It will never serve you positively to waste energy on any level trying to change what you cannot change.

As the famous serenity prayer says, "God grant me the serenity to accept the things I cannot change; courage to change the things I can; and wisdom to know the difference." Or, as the Buddhist teachings tell us, "It is our resistance to what is, that causes our suffering."

If we want to do away with money hardships, relationship problems, loneliness, sickness, guilt, unfulfilled desires, etc., we must be committed to detachment.

This includes detaching ourselves from people and how we expect them to behave. Instead of holding onto your idea of how things should be, allow yourself and those around you the freedom to be as they may. Detach yourself from certainties and allow yourself to be OK with uncertainty. Allow uncertainty to be part of your experience without holding onto any preconceived notions.

Become excited about the infinite possibilities that exist in the universe and know that everything happens for a reason so as you continue to journey towards manifesting your dreams, accepting what is and changing what you can keep you open to infinite choices.

CASH ADVANCE # 40
BECOME YOUR GOD-SELF

"I am here for a purpose and that purpose is to grow into a mountain, not to shrink to a grain of sand. Henceforth I will apply ALL my efforts to become the highest mountain of all and I will strain my potential until it cries for mercy."

– Og Mandino

As one of the earlier principles instructed you to "not" dim your light, this principle is about reaching a place of knowing that you are great and walking in it. This is the pinnacle of all of the principles because reaching this place says that no matter what happens, you are successful. You don't see failures, you don't see setbacks, you don't see loss. All you see, embrace, and focus on is greatness from the inside out. Nothing can shake you because you know who you are no matter what. Even a "fall from grace" wouldn't be enough to stop you because you know that everything is working for your greater good. When you reach this level, you don't believe in negative or positive, nor do you view things as good or bad because ALL of it is God and God is the Greatest, so God cannot make mistakes. You also have accepted that you are made in the image and likeness of God, which also makes you a god = Greatness on Display. But you also know that you are not the only god; you are a god amongst god's so if you have enlightened yourself enough to know this, your job becomes to exemplify this to others so that they too can believe in their god-self. I now understand my assignment and will continue to live my life to the fullest so that others can know that they can live their absolute best life no matter their circumstance! The best is yet to come, so I pray that you receive this message and move in excellence.

Below is a summary of The Science of Being Great by Wallace D Wattles that explains this concept in greater detail:

CRACKING THE CODE:

A Summary of The Science of Being Great

ALL men are made of the one intelligent substance, and therefore all contain the same essential powers and possibilities. Greatness is equally inherent in all and maybe manifested by all. Every person may become great. Every constituent of God is a constituent of man.

A man may overcome both heredity and circumstances by exercising the inherent creative power of the soul. If he is to become great, the soul must act and rule the mind and the body.

Man's knowledge is limited, and he falls into error through ignorance; he must connect his soul with the Universal Spirit to avoid this. Universal Spirit is the intelligent substance from which all things come; it is in and through all things.

All things are known to this universal mind, and man can so unite himself to enter into all knowledge.

To do this man must cast out of himself everything that separates him from God. He must will to live the divine life and rise above all moral temptations; he must forsake every course of action that is not in accord with his highest ideals.

He must reach the right viewpoint, recognizing that God is all, in all, and that there is nothing wrong. He must see that nature, society, government, and industry are perfect in their present stage and advancing toward completion; and that all men and women everywhere are perfect.

He must know that all's right with the world and unite with God for the completion of the perfect work. It is only as man sees God as the Great Advancing Presence in all and good in all that he can rise to real greatness.

He must consecrate himself to the service of the highest within himself,

obeying the voice of the soul. There is an Inner Light in every man that continuously impels him toward the highest, and this light must guide him if he would become great.

He must recognize the fact that he is one with the Father, and consciously affirm this unity for himself and for all others. He must know himself to be a god among gods, and act accordingly.

He must have absolute faith in his own perceptions of truth and begin to act upon these perceptions at home. As he sees the true and right course in small things, he must take that course. He must cease to act unthinkingly and begin to think; and he must be sincere in his thought.

He must form a mental conception of himself at the highest and hold this conception until it is his habitual thought-form of himself. This thought-form he must keep continuously in view. He must outwardly realize and express that thought-form in his actions.

He must do everything that he does in a great way. In dealing with his family, neighbors, acquaintances, and friends, he must make every act an expression of his ideal. The man who reaches the right viewpoint and makes full consecration, and who fully idealizes himself as great, and who makes every act, however trivial, an expression of the ideal, has already attained to greatness.

Everything he does will be done in a great way. He will make himself known, and will be recognized as a personality of power. He will receive knowledge by inspiration, and will know all that he needs to know.

He will receive all the material wealth he forms in his thoughts, and will not lack for any good thing. He will be given the ability to deal with any combination of circumstances that may arise, and his growth and progress will be continuous and rapid.

Great works will seek him out, and all men will delight to do him honor. Because of its peculiar value to the student of the Science of Being Great,

Ash Cash Deposit Ticket

Bank

2408 8TH AVENUE APT 1A
NEW YORK, NY 10027-1849

TRANSACTION #4

DATE *August 30, 2020*

ACCOUNT NO. **STATEMENT AUDIT**

Two Hundred Twenty Four Million

WRITE AMOUNT IN FULL ON ABOVE LINE

Ash Cash Exantus

SIGNATURE

The Financial Motivator

TITLE

DOLLARS $ | *$224,000,000*

The Most High GOD

APPROVED BY

ASH CASH EXANTUS

TRANSACTION #4
STATEMENT AUDIT

ACCOUNTS OF ASH'S LIFE AS TOLD BY THOSE CLOSEST TO HIM

BY NAADIRA BROWN

Wow! Where do I begin? Do I start with my name; what I do for a living; or, how I even came to be responsible for this Statement Audit? I am really at a loss for words, but eager to take you on my interview journey. As you read above, my name is Naadira Brown, the interviewer who was and still *is* in a complete state of shock that I was asked to take on a project such as this. Why, you ask? For starters, I am not an author. I am a retired Soldier. Second, I have never conducted interviews like the ones I did for this project. I have interviewed people for jobs. Third, this entire experience helped me to truly believe that God doesn't call the qualified; He qualifies the called. That means He has and will equip you with every single thing you need to do His work. Whatever your calling is, you are already successfully wired to achieve it. All you have to do is believe and be obedient and that is what I did every step of the way.

About a week prior to taking on this project, I was talking to a classmate about one of my favorite jobs ever – as a telemarketer! Imagine that! I don't remember how the conversation came about, but I was explaining that the reason I am so polite with telemarketers is because I used to be one. Sometimes you have to walk a mile in someone's shoes to really understand them. Well, when Ash asked me to work on this project, I said yes. I didn't even know what the project would entail at that time, but my answer was yes. I quickly learned that I would be receiving a list of names and numbers to call and speak with as I had when I was a telemarketer. This may not mean much to you, but I believe (and now know) it was God setting the stage for what would be a life-changing experience for me.

I conducted thirty-two interviews in a one-month time span and my life has been forever changed by each of them. I asked a series of four questions to which I told the interviewees to give their honest feedback, speak as long as they wanted and flow freely while I took notes. When they finished, I read back what I captured and asked if there was anything to add or take away. Let me just say, some of the people were guarded. They wondered who I was, what I wanted and why. Others were nervous, wondering if they should simply say "all the right things" or be honest. All in all, most were eager to share, and I felt like I had a new family member after each call. I experienced it all throughout this process– joy, inspiration, goosebumps, tears, honor, respect, encouragement and so much more. There were days I wanted to call Ash after each interview just to say, "Thank you again for allowing me to do this" or "So and so was so dope!" I was so excited just to hear each person say hello. I was happy each day I had an appointment to speak with an interviewee! I shed tears of joy! I laughed at the stories that were shared. To sum it up, I am eternally thankful for this experience and what made this even greater for me (personally) was the feedback I received after each interview. Again, not knowing that while I was receiving gifts to provide to Ash, I was unwrapping my own in the process. So, let's get started on this journey.

The questions are below, and the receipts will follow:

1. **Who is Ash Cash?**

2. **How is the man we all see today different or the same as when he was younger?**

3. **Can you tell me any story that sticks out to you that you remember about Ash?**

4. **Why is Ash's story important?**

AMINA PHELPS-EXANTUS (THE FIRST LADY)

"Ash, hmmm….if I could describe him in one word, it would be a unicorn or leprechaun. Basically, I would describe him as one of those figures that don't exist, but you believe in them anyway. Ash is the most unique person I've ever met in my lifetime. His mind, his thoughts, his analytical abilities and everything that make him up are summarized by one word – unique. I met Ash in his 20s and he is pretty much the same with the exception of being more mature (of course.) He's always been loud, outgoing and personable. He went from playful loud to purposeful loud. From the life of the party loud to life-changing loud. All in all, in present-day, Ash has a more defined goal and puts every ounce of his energy towards it. The story I'd share is how we met. Both of us worked at the bank. I was an avid reader and Ash noticed. One day, I was reading "Before the Mayflower" when Ash walked through the teller line. He pretended to be interested in the book I was reading and even went out and bought it (laughs.) Little did I know, he had a bet with another guy we worked with and used the book to get me out on a date and the rest is history. Ash's story is important because he has an opportunity to be a demonstration. Whether today or 10-15 years ago he was always a beacon of light. Coming from the same humble, rough beginnings and showing that there is another way. He has, is and will always uplift the community.

ROSALYN "ROZ" SMALLS (SISTER)

"Oh man! (laughs) It's so much I could say, but Ash in a nutshell is someone who's thoughtful. He takes to heart what people have to say. Ash as a little brother, always considered others. His heart was always so big. For him being a little kid with a heart like that was so special. His consideration is baffling especially for a child. He knew what to say when it needed to be said. He was protective of me and always had my back from then until now. His kindness transcended his age. It was always the two of us and we had each other's back. He was smaller than me in size at one point, but his heart was always larger than life and larger than his size. As for the man we see today, there's not much of a difference with him. The main difference is in his roles and responsibilities. He is more sculpted and formulated. He has defined his purpose and fully walked into it. He was growing then and doing what came naturally and now he does the same thing, but with intentions and full understanding behind it. He's more seasoned. There are so many stories, but one that resonates with me is that he was young and packing bags at the supermarket (Bravo across the street from where we lived.) He was always so eager and motivated to work. He was conscientious and saw the struggle my mom (and our family had) and he brought whatever he made to our mother. He was always so considerate that he'd run across with what money he had whether finished working or not and provide for us. His consideration and maturity was and will always be a part of any story I have about my brother. Ash's story is important to show his humility. How he cares. How his care and efforts go into everything he does. He is not selfish, he's selfless. This is important because he has been this way for his entire life and now that he has more of a reach, it is so imperative that his story is told. Truthfully, his kindness and humility is what got him where he is today despite the odds and the beginning of it all. His story is just WOW."

DANIEL NELSON (BROTHER)

"Ash is that person you can't refuse. You can't disregard him. You can't forget him. Ash is passion. He is life. He is a fighter that consistently wins. Ash is the same, but different because he's older, of course. His character has never changed. No matter what he sets his mind to, he will achieve. He's as humble now as he has always been. He's your best bottle of wine that has only gotten better with time. I'm his brother – of course I have stories. His goal was to get up and out of his circumstances and he did. He told me that he was about to retire, and I will never forget hearing those words. As shocking as they were, his drive to do it and actually getting it done is a story worth telling. The moment you tell him he can't do something, he does it twice and takes pictures. **Story**-during my detox phase, I shared with him that I wanted to do a podcast. His support was pivotal, critical and needed. I will never forget that. He's loud by passion, not by anger. Ash's story is important because if you see where he came from and what he was able to make of himself, it is a MUST tell. The struggle was really a struggle. The tough times were very tough. However, Ash stayed the course. The course that was actually the calling on his life – to inspire, motivate and encourage all that he came into contact with and now all that are within the sound of his voice. He matches energy only to transform it into Action, Success, Prosperity, Motivation and Greatness on Display."

ALINE BARRON (CHILDHOOD FAMILY FRIEND)

"First and foremost, Ash is my little brother. I am Roz's best friend, and our families grew up together. I remember Ash being so shy and seeing him outspoken is amazing. I am inspired by him every day. Ash was always shy. His mom was always praying for him. She saw his potential and kept pushing him to greatness. I am amazed and not much has changed – from his values and willingness to help and now he's living it all out loud. Hmmm (laughs) a story about Ash…when we were smaller, we were always together. We had our birthdays and went to church together. We were bonded by so much and it was always funny that Ash was the only boy amongst all of us girls. Ash's story is important because where he is now really tells us all that we can make it. In particular, his community. Our community. People of color. His dedication to teaching others about finance to break out of the shackles of debt is awe inspiring. He continues to elevate, while keeping it real and being his authentic self. He's mastered the boardroom and the streets. His passion translates in all that he does and it's so beautiful. No age barriers. No excuses. Let's get to it. He also shines as a husband, businessman and father. He's inspiring us all in more ways than one. Like in every single aspect of life."

JASMINE BERNARD-STRAKER
(CHILDHOOD FAMILY FRIEND)

"Ash (laughing) to me, is my brother. He is a person that I watched grow into a man, husband, father and motivator. He is an inspiration to so many including me. He didn't use his past as a weakness, but as his strength. As far as how he's changed or remained the same, Ash has always had drive and a good head on his shoulders. What you see today is his heightened confidence and presence. I love how he became a much better version of himself turning all negatives to positives. In sharing stories, Ash was always a fighter (laughs). There were these twin girls that we grew up with that Ash used to pick on and one day they had enough, and they were trying to jump him. I wasn't having that and jumped in. This was in the 1st grade and Ash wound up getting kicked out of school because everyone knew that he started it. It's funny to think about now, but the truth is, I will always have his back. Ash loves hats. He always had a collection of them around his room and Jay-Z was always blasting. Another funny memory I'd like to share is how Ash used to cut up hot dogs, fry them and eat them with ketchup. I laugh now, but I have cooked the same thing and now my children cook it. There are so many stories I could share, but Ash having my back and making others feel safe will always be a part of them. Ash's story is important because a lot of people that can easily be overlooked can see themselves in him. His relatability shines through and illuminates inspiration. His story is needed for people of color and people from the hood (of course,) but I believe any and every one can see themselves in him."

MASTER UNIVERSE (CHILDHOOD FRIEND)

"NY in the 80s and 90s was the mecca and still is, but back then, the environment of absentee fathers and poverty were just a couple of the things that Ash and I shared. We went to the same school and church and our families were connected. He was my brother. I didn't even get into ½ the trouble that Ash did, yet in *my* mother's eyes, Ash could do no wrong. Back then, he was mischievous, although he was smart. Ash got suspended at every level including day care! He would not tolerate disrespect from anyone. Today, he has left his mischief behind and consistently demonstrates his educated side. I have so many stories I could share, but I will keep it short – Ash put Leo down on sight. Leo was a kid we went to school with that used to bully others. Although Ash had just come off suspension, Leo decided to test Ash and that was it. Ash knocked him out! I believe Ash was more upset about the fight being stopped than the fact that Leo had attempted to bully him. Ash's story is important because a lot of us didn't make it out. I cry inside thinking about Ash. As people grow, sometimes you realize they aren't who they say they are, but Ash proves that authenticity is key. Despite the poverty of the times (80s and 90s), Ash not only came up, he got out and remained true to who he was. He proves that nice guys don't always finish last."

MARQUISE "QUISE" HARDIN (CHILDHOOD FRIEND)

"Oh wow (laughs), there's no one answer for who Ash is. I grew up with him, so it's really hard to say one thing. Our relationship spans growing up, adulthood, mentorship, you name it. He's always been a leader who encouraged positivity and the mindset of getting it done. He's never been afraid to show the good and bad – an authentic leader to say the least. Ash has always been attentive. He consistently pays attention and simplifies the biggest lessons into scenarios and terminology we all can understand. Ash and I grew up in St. Nick projects. His mother was very religious, and I can remember Ash's room window faced the loading dock. We could see him through his window and on a particular occasion Ash was on punishment and couldn't come outside. We played Nintendo with him through his window for hours. Ash's story is important because it touches so many levels – poverty, wealth, college, book writing. His story gives hope beyond measure. His story is our story because he gives us something to aspire to. Ash has taken every up and down in stride, never leaving out or reducing any part. It is all worthy and will be forever. One more thing, I remember the first DVD player came to Blockbuster and Ash was the first to have one. He was always ahead."

ANGEL "A-ROCKS" PORTER (CHILDHOOD FRIEND)

"Ash is a lot of things to me, but first and foremost he is my childhood best friend. He lived in 2406 and I lived in 2410. We were a crew and a team and while we are still those things to one another, Ash was always about the collective. He always shared information and remained thankful for all things. He was the first person I met and grew up with from the Caribbean. His family was like my family, and I knew them all. Ash was smart. He was the first from our crew with a real job and overall, he was the day brightener. His voice, its inflection and his spirit were some of the traits I remember and cherish most. In Ash's younger days (like the ages of 8-10), he was quiet amongst a crowd. He gradually opened up through his basketball skills. His skills gave him a new sense of "talk shit-ability" which also honed in on his gift of being able to encourage or discourage others with his words. This contributes directly to the man we see today who knows the power of his tongue and uses it wisely. Seeing Ash go from rags to riches as far as clothing is one thing, but his spirit has never changed. His influence was invaluable in the elevation of us all. His giving nature is and will always be present and his use of teachable moments are endless. A story I remember about Ash…(laughs) is centered around brotherhood. We were in a summer youth program and played basketball games together. Back in the day we both had a Sony walkman and met up to hang out as usual. The Nas album had come out and we used to count to three simultaneously in order to press play at the same time and bounce on beat in unison even though we were listening on different devices. Ash was never stingy and basketball was life. The park we played ball in was on 128th and 7th Ave. We were being talked to by an OG about going to play ball out in LeFrak City (Queens), yet Ash was the leader that encouraged us all to go along instead of staying in the streets of where we lived. Ash's story is important for many reasons. He comes from an immigrant family who endured many struggles yet overcame them all. He was a young, poor kid who went from the projects to what we now see in the world – a mogul and an inspiration. I will never forget that after my own father served 32 years in prison, Ash was the one who helped him write a book; therefore, not just being an inspiration to his own family, but others and even the world."

COREY "CO" CARTER (CHILDHOOD FRIEND)

"Ash is a childhood friend of mine. He's one of my best friends and our building 2406 is not only where we lived, but where it all began. Ash has made big improvements, but his go-getter mindset has always been the same. We went from playing on the monkey bars and playing basketball to working, but Ash found what he loved and never stopped elevating. He went from doing knucklehead things as a kid with boundaries, to the man of excellence we see today without limits as to what he can achieve. There are a bunch of stories I could share, but I remember him helping me get one of my 1st jobs. The job was at Blockbuster Video and helped me and another one of our friends, Kamel. The main takeaway from this story is Ash showing that there were other ways to get out. One more story that comes to mind was when we were playing basketball on the monkey bars, and I tried to dunk on Ash. Being much taller than me, I fell into his arms and my nose started bleeding. Ash carried me inside and although he hadn't done anything to intentionally hurt me, his mom was on my side and upset with him. Ash's story is important because it speaks for itself and so many others. I'd call him the Chosen One. We came up in the projects, yet Ash's mentality superseded his environment. He can speak to choosing the hard right over the easy wrong. Simply put, Ash's story speaks for a lot of people. "

KAMEL "MEL" ROBINSON (CHILDHOOD FRIEND)

"Ash and I grew up together and we always looked out for each other like we were brothers. Ash is 100% different which is to be expected. He has progressed so much. A lot of us didn't make it out and he did. He was way ahead of his time and saw the business aspect and used that to create change. He decided to be the change and has stayed positive. He helped us all then and continues to now. Ash always believed in me even when I didn't believe in myself. He got me my first legal job at Blockbuster videos and years later when I became a personal trainer, he helped me create my company Flippin Weight, which is the business that I have today. There are too many stories to count, but the one that really sticks out to me is when Ash was at Seward Park High School and one day he jumped the turnstile and got arrested. He was crying and so upset, thinking he'd never get a good job, his life was ruined, he wouldn't have a good life, and so on. Later on, when he was trying to become a banker, they asked about his background. He was honest on his application, and I asked why he did that since the situation was not on his record. It was funny to me, but thankfully that did not hinder Ash in any way. Ash's story is important because he is always progressing. He's always helping. He preaches how to go from one level to the next and always over delivers. He gives you the whole package at a fraction of the cost. Ash's story shows how you can finance yourself, grow your business, and become a brand for your own life as an entrepreneur. Ash's story has made my story."

DEDRIC "BELOVED" HAMMOND (CHILDHOOD FRIEND)

"Who is Ash Cash? is a good question. I always saw Ash as a young, modest brother. In the hood with gangstas and crime, Ash was respected without being in that life. He was unique and okay with just being himself. I truly treasure Ash and who he is. As for differences, I'd say there is only one; Ash was on the verge of choosing the wrong path, but I was like his protector. He was young and well-rounded and has been able to maintain that. The way he loved then and now is the same, but there is no way he'd take a chance with his life as he almost did in that moment. The story I'd like to share represents how we stayed connected. I used to have Ash hold money for me. It's funny because I know Ash used to wonder "why me?" I was connected to the streets, but Ash was my safe haven. I advised Ash to stick with the bank and his legal jobs. I remember Ash came on the block once and he was venting about a situation. I asked for the address of where his "problem" was. He knew we didn't play about him and that day I believe was when he learned a valuable lesson – if it ain't that serious, don't talk about it. Fast-forward to now, Ash knows who had his back then and will have it forever. Ash's story is important because he's one of those guys. People always like to say you are a product of your environment, yet he is NOT. His story shows that he can be right where we are (in poverty) and still overcome. What I pull most from his story is that Ash is a believer. When God told me, Beloved, sell your books and you are overlooking your talents, I was able to call Ash to share. I also asked Ash to tell his story at a program I was working at. What Ash said back then was and continues to be necessary. Everyone in the projects ain't hood and his story proves that you do not have to be a product of your environment to be powerful, respected and live out your purpose. ``

ULYSSES "RICH KID" MCCRAY
(CHILDHOOD EMPLOYER + OG)

"Ash Cash is family, my little brother. Family forever. Harlem is family and depending on your background (drugs, fatherless, abuse), you find your family and we fill the voids and needs of one another. His thirst was recognized early on and never left. I am beyond proud of him. He's the next billionaire – Reginald Lewis, Robert Smith. It costs nothing to be kind, educate and share. Ash did and continues to do just that. Ash's demeanor was always respectful, nice and pleasant. His eagerness to learn was always present, but now he can share it effectively with others. He's taken the roots of the hood and made it the tree of knowledge. He can bloom anywhere he's planted – whether with CEO's or in the neighborhood. It is a humbling experience to be a vendor and I can remember the way Ash never allowed his self-esteem to be challenged by being one. Some people's image, pride and ego take over, but Ash's never did. He took pride in simply being of service and kept his smile no matter what. His story is important because he's my hero. My superhero. We all need superheroes. Ash is a hero of color – his skin, complexion, intellect, impact, wealth amassed and so on show that we can do what he's doing and who doesn't need that? God has given him the platform and he's using it positively and effectively. I am in awe of him and who he's become. Knowing he came from where he came from, is where he's at and can go further is awe inspiring. He's given back to society more than society has ever given him. That's why he's a hero. My hero. He tells us all that we can be so much more and that's why his story is important."

AQIL DAVIDSON FROM THE LEGENDARY HIP-HOP GROUP "WRECKX-N-EFFECT" (CHILDHOOD OG)

"How can I put this...Ash Cash is a shining example of what's possible coming from where possibilities seem impossible. He has navigated the whirlwind of his surroundings and came out on top. Very few have made it out, and Ash is one. He's been able to break the norm, so in short, he has had the perseverance of what it took and takes to get out. There's been more than not, a consistency of vibrance, good energy, and a spirit of excellence from Ash. His energy and spirit have consistently been a light. I'd say the only difference is the power of his light from one year to the next – one age to the next – and one challenge to the next. One story in particular comes to mind that I remember about Ash: in my process on the way up with music, I had my set-up in my family house (the living room.) Once, I needed several people for a background crowd effect on a hook and I rounded up Ash and some others and the person I remember MOST is ASH. With all the yelling and the crowd effect that I needed, clearly Ash was who made the difference. Ash's story is important for one reason: Introspect. His story is important from the perseverance aspect, but I've also watched his stages of growth. Those stages show progression. This display, or example, is needed for those that come from where he comes from and he fills the void of who we need. Who his community needs. Who we all need. He is a beacon of light of productivity, possibility, hope and promise. Personally, Ash's story means the world to me. I pay it forward with what he has strengthened and empowered me with and that is priceless. As I worked inwardly, I had (and have) Ash's support, knowledge, encouragement and inspiration. Ash, his story and our personal relationship is like the big gun that we all need to pull out sometimes."

SAM DOUGLAS
(CHILDHOOD BASKETBALL COACH + OG)

"Ash is your typical guy from the hood. Projects raised. He ran with the crowd, but he knew he needed to make better decisions. He pivoted and made changes for the better that would impact his life forever. At a younger age, Ash was a good follower, but eventually he came into his true position as a leader. He had left a mark at the lower level and is now making his mark at the highest levels. He's the same in that he was and is the go-to guy to get things done. When Ash was a young teen, I worked at the police athletic league (PAL) and he and his crew came with their attitudes and I wasn't having it. The exchange we had way back then has bridged the gap to where we are today which is a relationship of mutual love and respect. Ash's story is important for the simple fact that we have so many adults that never grew up. They fall into ignorance too easily, especially when it comes to finance. Ash is teaching financial literacy and his story is important to be an example for us to emulate. He shows the HOW and all we have to do is follow the blueprint."

GREG "F-MOS" HOLLEY (CHILDHOOD FRIEND)

"I met Ash at the age of 14 years old and have known him for many years. He's an authentic human being and has grown to be such an innovator both personally and professionally. Personally, he has a unique skill to elevate others like he did when we collaborated on Street Heat. Professionally, he is always looking at what we can do next or bigger. His hallmarks are energy, innovation and authenticity. The man you all see today in comparison to who he was years ago hasn't changed much. From his first banking job at Chase Bank to now translating business to our community in a language we understand, he has always been motivated to learn and share knowledge with others. I'd say a difference at one point was him being closed off as if what he was doing in banking and finance lived on a resume, but he completely elevated it ALL from the resume to real life. Another difference is seeing him in his roles as a husband and father. As for a story I remember, our label, Street Heat was ground-breaking for our neighborhood. Ash was always the type to get things done which was proven when he used his Kinko's job to print all of the promo material that we needed. He took everything he did to the MAX and consistently sought elevation. He'd rather ask forgiveness than permission when it came to getting things done. I remember when his first book came out and I popped up in the Bronx to show support at his book signing. I saw Ash talking to maybe two or three people one on one. He was sincerely dedicated to excellence, elevation and encouragement. Ash is by far one of the strongest financial minds in the black community. His story is important because it is the quintessential kid from the hood makes good and comes back - the real version, not the fake one. He has taken all that he learned, remixed it and brought it back in a way that his community understands, wants to hear and will accept. Many people have this (rags to riches) story, but the abundance he reached makes his story critical. As a Haitian-American who flipped so little into so much makes him a man that must be known. "

JAB UNO (OG)

"Ash is my little brother (laughs.) Ash has always had the same core character – a learner, learns from everything, doesn't need to feel the fire to know it's hot as he will take notes from those who've gone before him. There is no change because I could always see where Ash was going and that was up. As for stories to share, I mainly kept Ash out of stuff. Myself and some of the others in our neighborhood were doing things that would *create* stories, yet, we knew Ash was greater than our surroundings so we didn't want him involved. I might tell him some things, but never wanted him to be a part of it for his own good. I can remember a time that I took Ash to the Cheetah Club and he was buggin' because of how we were treated like royalty by security and those who worked at the club. He thought that was crazy and I guess you can say that's about the craziest thing I let him be a part of. Ash always called me his mentor, but really he was the one schooling me. The student became the teacher in our case. Ash's story is important because he's a perfect example of not letting anything hold you back. He came from the bottom and stayed the course even when he had many curve balls thrown at him. I believe his BIG energy is what has allowed him to succeed BIG. Ash is like a ghetto blueprint – he came from the bottom and let his energy and mindset carry him up and out."

KIMBO
(CHILDHOOD FRIEND + STREET HEAT PARTNER)

"Ash is a guy I grew up with, but he's more than that. He's someone I've watched grow into someone who's always ready. From our label, Street Heat to where he is now, he's always been ready. I can see him taking on the world, project by project of any size and magnitude. Ash is the same today as when we were younger. He used to freestyle and was always quick on his feet – same as today. He has naturally matured, but like I said, he was and is always ready. He used what he has always done to master whatever he needs to accomplish. A story I remember, but not sure if he does, was one time I borrowed his bike. I literally had his bike from early in the day until late that evening. I had gone all the way downtown and everything. Ash was so upset. Ash's story is important because he shows what you can become if you put your mind to it. He comes from the same environment as so many, yet rose above adversity. His story shows that there is so much more out there, you just have to go and get it."

DJ GET ON UP (
CHILDHOOD FRIEND + STREET HEAT PARTNER)

"Ash Cash is my brother. We came up together. I gave him the name King of Finance since we had given the preface "king" to so many other things (laughs.) We started a record label called Street Heat and Ash was and still is ambitious. From then until now, his ambition has multiplied x 20,000 although it was very strong even in his younger years. Whatever Ash put his mind to, he always got done which is still the same today. It is amazing to see his growth as a great dad and husband, too! I have so many stories I could share, but this one sticks out most: Ash could have been promoted to Bank President when we started our record label, but he sacrificed it all for our label. He got a job at FEDEX/Kinkos and used that connection to print flyers and whatever we needed to promote our label. His belief in me, us and Street Heat will forever stick out to me. Finally, Ash's story is important because he's a kid from St. Nick projects and while the battle we all had to endure was big, nothing got in his way. He is an inspiration to me and I learned not to let anything get in my way as well. We had it rough, but Ash got out. Despite being around people doing the wrong things, I always knew Ash was going to do something big. He has been sending motivational quotables since the MySpace era and I remember Jermaine Dupri catching wind of it as well. Ash and his ability to motivate and inspire has always been a part of who he is."

KEV STARKS
(CHILDHOOD FRIEND + STREET HEAT PARTNER)

"Simply put, Ash is that dude. My guy. We go back at least 16, 17 years and Ash has always had the same energy and been a good person. There is no change in that aspect, but watching him grow into a husband and father are really the only differences. A story that I recall had to do with our record label, Street Heat, which consisted of myself, DJ Get On Up, FMOS, Kimbo and Ash. We were doing an event in Times Square and we needed flyers. Ash printed like 10,000 of them at his Kinkos job with our DJ's face on them and we literally had them all over the place! You couldn't even see the ground once all the flyers had fallen. I will never forget how much he believed in our record label. Ash's story is important because his energy is so dope and inspiring. Everyone needs to see and hear his story because nobody makes it out of St. Nick projects and he did. That alone makes his story worth sharing! His inspiration is helping others and the outreach is needed for all of us. Most recently his wife, Amina did a Black History Month education series and that was super dope as well!"

TAQIY MUHAMMAD (HIGH SCHOOL FRIEND)

"Ash Cash is the definition of life. He is life. He's vibrant. His energy and presence encompasses all that he is. Positivity. Influence. Black excellence. Pure alignment. Our relationship started in 10th grade and his infectious personality was/is the same. The evolution of Ash is now a direct correlation of spiritual law of attraction principles in his business. My story I'd like to share about Ash only has 3 words – Brooklyn Versus Harlem! (Mase Versus Jay-Z) I remember when Ash saw the light after gaining an understanding of how much Jay-Z had impacted his own life. Ash's story is important because it's a story that our people can relate to. It takes trials and tribulations infused with success and the desire to not only reach, but surpass your potential. Finally, Brooklyn Stand Up! No further comments.

HECTOR GARCIA (HIGH SCHOOL FRIEND)

"Ash Cash is my brother and one of my dearest friends. He's an inspiration to me in many ways, but especially when it comes to finance. Personally, I think he is more focused and driven. I've known Ash for over 20 years and I've literally watched him live his goals out loud. Whatever he sets out to do, he gets it done and that hasn't changed. I remember Ash used to work in a bank in Harlem (144th St) and I was going through a tough time with budgeting my own money. I asked Ash for help. He itemized my finances and taught me how to budget my money. It spoke to me then and continues to be a part of my money relationship to this day. Ash's story is important because it's relatable. From poor to more. The relatability of his story is inspiration and motivation. Furthermore, in the inner city, you see sports or negative activities as a way to make money. Ash shows that there are other ways to be successful which is why his story is important. It's relatability at its finest.

TANGIE WALLACE
(BLOCKBUSTER VIDEOS CO-WORKER + SISTER)

"Ash Cash is the most delightful person you'd ever want to know. His energy makes the quietest person want to open up. The difference from then to now is how Ash has grown with experience; but what has remained the same is his intellect and energy. Ash is like my little brother. I remember working with him at Blockbuster years ago. He was always playing music and singing. He was the first to introduce me to the artist Juvenile and his song "Ha" which I still think of Ash til' this day when I hear it. I honestly have so many stories I could tell, but the main memory of Ash I'd like to share is that I've never seen him be anything but joyful which is such a rare trait. Finally, Ash's story is important for so many reasons. As a black, young male, he is literally educating and taking over the world encouraging others (young and old) to read, where otherwise they might not have; he's making a positive impact in the black community; and he comes from the projects and has made it so far.``

EDWIN CINTRON (MANAGER AT BLOCKBUSTER
VIDEOS + CITIBANK 🖋)

"Wow! (laughs) Hmmmm, that's tough. I met Ash coming out of high school; we worked at Blockbuster together maybe 25 years ago. Wow. He is definitely someone who's self-motivated, a go-getter and such an active and positive person. Probably more positive than anyone I've ever worked with. I tune in to Ash's show sometimes, but I knew he'd always be a go-getter, that hasn't changed over time. I grew up in the struggle as well. The person we see today is a great father and family man. He has really done well. Seeing him, a jokester and his huge personality, (smart, motivated, etc.) is the same but him as a family man is amazing. A story I'd like to share is when Ash asked me to come back to banking while I was still managing operations. The great story was the way Ash brought one of the bank branches from the bottom to the top. This branch struggled to meet their goals and Ash raised them to be ranked #1 in the area within 1 year! He inspired the entire staff and that made me so proud. He facilitated the reward of a complimentary iPad for the staff, which was great, although he didn't give me one…(laughs) Ash's story is important because it shows that no matter your age or circumstance, you can do whatever you want. With inspiration and motivation, you can't lose and Ash's story shows that."

JACKIE MARRIOTT
(MENTOR AND COLLEAGUE AT CHASE BANK)

"Who is Ash Cash, you say? Hmmm, he is a person that is willing to learn and absorbs info. He never gets upset. He looks out for others, is caring and very talented. I told him, the sky's the limit and he's actually taken that and ran with it. As for what is the same or different, there are some differences. He grew up. Grasped every lesson and learned from it. He grew and got better. He never stayed where he started – his attitude of never staying down has stuck with him. Ash said to me when he was younger that he wanted to retire and he did it. He never stopped then and continues putting his best foot forward with all that he wants. A story I'd like to share is about his retirement at 30 at the 40/40 club. Another was when he was a teller. His eloquent way of speaking, working and being was relatable and impactful. He elevated into a family man, husband and father whose presence could always be felt. The belief he had and has in himself is present in any story related to Ash. He consistently dressed for the part he wanted, not the part he had. Ash's story is important because everybody should know where he came from, where he's been and where he's going. His story is an example for even those that have taught him something because learning and growing is forever. Ash has truly embodied the gift of drive, motivation and inspiration. His ability of putting in the time and work and most importantly – Belief in SELF is worthy of ALL to KNOW, read, hear and witness. Nothing happens before its time as long as God wants it to happen. Everything happens in God's time and this is Ash's time."

ERICA LEWIS (COLLEAGUE AT CHASE BANK)

"I have one request – that I receive an autographed copy of his book when it's released! So, who is Ash Cash? (laughs) When I met Ashley Exantus, who is now Ash Cash, we were coworkers at Chase. He was ambitious, focused on what he wanted from finance, likeable, yet respected by his client base. He was focused on getting things done. He elevated, while staying grounded. He went to another black owned bank after leaving Chase – always looking for more, but doesn't keep it to himself. Ash truly passes the baton. He embodies determination, humility, authenticity and transparency. Ash has grown into the man he is today. His eagerness was and is the same. You never outgrow knowledge. Education and God always remained his foundation. He is changing the game from his West Indian Culture (the past) blended intimately with who he is today. He's grown in so many ways and the major growth is as a man, husband and father. Ash is younger than me and came to me discussing his feelings for Amina one day. They had separated, but seemed as if they wanted to get back together. My advice was to try again. Later on, hearing of them not only reconnecting, but getting married was and still is a blessing. Ash talked differently before marriage and children; yet, seeing him snap right into his role as a father and husband was a sight to see. Ash's story is important because of the year we've had (2020.) We need more men like Ash (Haitian, West Indian) out there. We (people of color) aren't heard from with the exception of negativity or something brief. Ash's story is timeless, yet motivating. Today's generation is entitled and Ash shows the work. Think about a math problem…he shows the work. He consistently shows the average person that they can do it too! Ash is the epitome of determination."

Interesting fact: He still has a love of cheese – mozzarella, cream, swiss, you name it (laughs)

DJ KUT (BIG BRO + INDUSTRY ✍)

"WOW! A simple, but hard question. Ash Cash is a genius. A true example of when you hear the saying: build it and they will come. Ash is the same. He is the same exact person. I can til this day call or text him and get a response. He is attentive. Caring. He gives knowledge, desires knowledge and uplifts his people. He is NOT Hollywood. He has grown right before my eyes (our eyes) and I am proud to see him reap what he has sown in abundance. I don't even know how I ended up on his list of getting the Daily Word, but I am thankful that I am. That's actually how it all began. It was motivation from thin air, cyberspace at a time that I needed it most. I reached out to Ash after DJ Carl Blaze got killed (Power 105) and after reading one of his Daily Word emails. I wondered if he knew Carl Blaze based on how in tune his message was that particular day. That's when our interactions began. Ash's story is important for one reason. I'll never forget when he did his retirement party at age 30. He did it at the 40/40 club. I didn't think it was crazy, but instead BRAVE. Watching his determination, motivation, re-invention and growth has been amazing. He is selfless, ever-growing and his blueprint is worthy of emulation by his community. His life is like a T.V. show that we can all star in."

MIKE "COBAINE IVORY" MCFADGEN
(FRIEND + SPIRITUAL ADVISOR)

"I would say, Ash is a ball of energy, positively motivating and a motivated person. He's a friend and of course known as the financial literacy expert to most. I don't have much experience with younger Ash, but we connected through his Daily Word. I reached out to him about a project and we discovered how like-minded we were. We have remained in contact over the last 10 years and nothing has changed except opportunity. He has been and continues to be a positive, energy filled, driven person. A story that sticks out to me was a time we played basketball together and Ash told everyone he was Baby Shaq. Each time we talk, it's as if the moments are always in alignment. Our timing is always right on time. Everyone loves the ashy to classy story (no pun intended), but from his humble beginnings he has been able to become tremendously successful. His story shows that no matter where you're from you can succeed and him remaining the same and true to himself definitely makes his story worth telling."

DAGOBERTO VELASQUEZ (FRIEND + MENTEE)

"Ash is my family; my older brother; a legend. We share a birthday, but he's ten years older than me. He has always motivated me and I wouldn't be where I am today without him. He is my go-to person for anything! He is humble, down to earth and a genius! Although Ash has grown a lot, his mindset is the same. A major difference from then to now, is that he has a wider audience. He's always wanted to make sure everyone's Mind was Right and he's always been a hustler. I have so many stories I could share, but I'll stick with the two that stand out most to me. I met Ash at Carver Bank. While conducting a transaction, my card was declined and I will never forget Ash swiping his card to come to my aid. Another story was when Ash invited me to a podcast (Dusse Friday w/Rel Carter) that he was doing, but thought that I could benefit from being in the room as well. Ash was always thinking about others. He told me to meet him downtown and make sure I had a thumb drive with my music on it. Little did I know, and to my surprise, I'd see Memphis Bleek! I also saw Biggs Burke briefly and I felt like a kid in a candy store! Ash didn't have to know my aspirations for him to pull me into an opportunity and this experience changed my life! Ash is an angel to me. Ash's story is important because we came from the same neighborhood and Ash shows that getting out is possible. He shows people that if you work hard, you can have whatever you want. I was at the bottom with him and have been able to witness Mind Right Money from where it was to where it is. Ash has overcome and brought so many people along."

MARK "MG" GOLDSMITH
(FOUNDER OF GETTING OUT & STAYING OUT)

"Ash is who he is. He has never changed. He's always been enthusiastic, knowledgeable and eager to share what he knows. He was always doing something and proves that when people think they are busy, oftentimes they are not productive. Ash embodies being busy, yet productive. Although I haven't known Ash very long, I can say that I've always seen his eagerness to share information with others. He's not just a sounding board but has consistently been someone who adds value to any space he's entered. He operates in the return on investment (ROI) space which is what I respect most. I met Ash through my company GOSO, and he was eager to go to Rikers Island to teach the young men at C74 how to Get Out and Stay Out (pun intended.) He was so natural with the young men and they respected what he had to say. His dedication to his community is why I would say his story is so important. He is an example for many to follow.

JEAN ALERTE (FRIEND)

"For me, Ash is a brother. Family. He's a necessity. He is needed for the purpose God put him here for. He is necessary. I see Ash as a sharper version of himself today than he was in the past. He hasn't changed very much because he always loved inspiring others from his friends to family. The difference is simply his reach. His family and friends were blessed to experience him sooner and now his gift has gone global. I'd like to share how we met. I can tell you specifically when it was. Egypt Sherard from HGTV asked us to sit on a board. We had never met, but when he came into the room, he brought the thunder. He began to speak and our characters mirrored. Haitian – check; Banker – check; Author of a book on inspiration –

check! We were and are one. We were connected before we ever connected. His book was Mind Right Money Right and my book was Do Right Do Good. At this point, the only difference was he was from Harlem and I was from Brooklyn. Ash's story is important because it's our story. It's everybody's story. Everyone can relate to feeling like a space is oversaturated, their story doesn't matter, shyness, or fear, but Ash shows that aside from the blue check and being verified, he is real. He is from where I'm from and shows where I can be. He is the demonstration of perseverance. The true product of consistency – through the ups and downs, the wins and losses, his desire and courage to still push is why his story is important."

ALFRED EDMOND
(MENTOR + SVP AT BLACK ENTERPRISE)

"Ash Cash is an authentic connector, an authentic educator and someone with great credibility and relatability because of his expertise. The Ash that I know today has been polished and pruned by life experiences that have made him more effective at reaching people where they are. It's one thing to be young and ambitious, but now he has been groomed from his own disruptions and meets people where they are just the same. The person that can help when your plans aren't working can help you better than the person whose plans have always worked. We did an event called SOAR in ATL in partnership w/TD Jakes enterprises. It was a one-day event that was more like a once in a lifetime ASH CASH SHOW. His relatability, authenticity and way of encouraging others was a story all in itself. He was truly greatness on display. He connected with everyone in the room because of his gift-which is simply being himself. Ash's story is important because it can minister to others with their own stories. The way he tells the story is as if the main character is the person he's speaking to and not himself. He is a mirror showing our challenges as simple speed-bumps in life that we can overcome. He does his work with joy, passion and authenticity, which is contagious.

Believing what he's doing and liking what's he's doing go hand in hand which is a blessing."

Note Naadira's fav part was when Alfred said: I'd never say that, that's cheesy. LMBO!!! It was when I added a line saying Ash "soared" at the SOAR event. Alfred said to take that part out...lol

TRU PETTIGREW (BIG BRO + SPIRITUAL ADVISOR)

"Ash is my brother. He's a source of inspiration for many. He's an amazing husband and father and purpose-driven professional. He has made it his mission to impact all the lives that he touches. The energy Ash possesses has always been the same. What you see is what you get. The energy, drive and motivation are transferred every time I talk to him. He's always been such an amazing source of energy and that has never changed. He accomplishes whatever he sets out to do. Ash spoke at a church in NC. He came to visit and I remember him sharing a story that was so transparent and vulnerable. Faith and finances was the topic and Ash's ability to connect through his authenticity was amazing and admirable. He shared that he was about to lose his house, yet as accomplished as he was, sharing something like this ensured the connection was ever-present. He encouraged others to never give up as he hadn't. He gave the audience what they needed at the expense of himself and his own pride. Ash's story is important because it gives hope. It lets people know that challenges and adversities may arise, but perseverance and resilience are what got him to where he is and can be the same for us. He is the demonstration of faith and hope that we all need which is why his story is important."

Ash Cash Deposit Ticket

Bank

TRANSACTION #5

2406 8TH AVENUE APT 1A
NEW YORK, NY 10027-1849

DATE _April 17, 2020_

ACCOUNT NO. **ADDITIONAL DEPOSITS**

DOLLARS $ | _$444,000,000_ |

Four Hundred Forty Four Million
WRITE AMOUNT IN FULL ON ABOVE LINE

The Most High GOD
APPROVED BY

Ash Cash Exantus
SIGNATURE

The Financial Motivator
TITLE

ASH CASH EXANTUS

BOOKS BY ASH CASH

MIND RIGHT, MONEY RIGHT

Mind Right, Money Right: 10 Laws of Financial Freedom, is a book designed to teach you how to effectively manage your personal finances. It shows you how having the right mental attitude and with laser sharp focus, you can have anything you desire in life. It's an easy to read book that anyone, at any level, can understand. The book's aim is to teach you these 10 proven Laws of Financial Freedom using the stories of wealthy men and women who have used them. This book is especially geared towards anyone who is tired of having a dependency on money and is ready to take some practical steps in order to correct it. Money is power but knowing how to make it work for you is freedom; Mind Right, Money Right will teach you how.

HUSSLENOMICS

Nipsey Hussle born Ermias Joseph Asghedom is often sited as a rapper and songwriter from Los Angeles, California but he was much more than that. Nipsey was a visionary, entrepreneur, community organizer, real estate investor, cryptocurrency enthusiast, activist, mentor, and so much more. Through his business moves, music, and community activism he was on a mission to teach his community about being fiscally responsible and owning your now and future in order to build wealth. On March 31, 2019, Nipsey was fatally shot outside his store, Marathon Clothing, and while it may have seemed that he died on that day, the truth is that Nipsey will live FOREVER! HussleNomics is a book dedicated to the legacy and teachings of Mr. Hussle with a step by step guide on how to implement each principle in your life. Nipsey often preached about the Marathon and as you know in a marathon the baton is often passed to the next runner to pick up where the other left off... HussleNomics is that baton! Long Live Nipsey Hussle! This is just the beginning!

THE WAKE UP CALL

The Wake Up Call: Financial Inspiration Learned from 4:44 + A Step by Step Guide on How to Implement Each Financial Principle, is a book designed to teach African-Americans how to manage money more effectively and how to build generational wealth. Jay-Z's 4:44 is the blueprint to bridging the wealth gap & solving economic inequalities for African-Americans! Through deciphering all of the financial concepts delivered within the album, readers will be taught about: • How to Build Credit to Use as Leverage • How to Spend Money Wisely • Cooperative Economics and How to Start a Business • Creating Multiple Streams of Income • How to Invest Money in Order For it To Grow • How to Pass Down Wealth to the Next Generation

MIND RIGHT, LIFE RIGHT

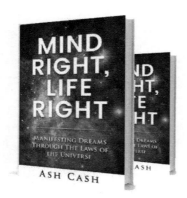

The Law of Attraction is arguably the most powerful law in the universe and over the past 10+ years many people have been realizing its power, especially with the introduction of The Secret. But what if I told you that it wasn't the only law? And if you only utilize the Law of Attraction you will be disappointed when your dreams aren't materializing? Mind Right, Life Right: Manifesting Your Dreams Through the Laws of the Universe is a book written to help those who are seeking true enlightenment, learn how to turn their dreams into reality. Through the nine Mindset Principles, readers will learn that the Law of Attraction is just a piece of the puzzle (although a big piece), and that if you combine this law with the other powerful principles that govern the universe, you can achieve ANYTHING you put your mind, grind and focus towards.

WHAT THE FICO

What the FICO: 12 Steps To Repairing Your Credit is the only credit repair book you'll ever need. It is a simple guide that will give you step-by-step instruction on how to go from bad to good credit in no time and minimal cost. If you follow these simple steps you are going to begin the journey of getting your credit and financial life back in order. This book is mainly for those who have tried to learn the credit game and have done so unsuccessfully but can also be used by those who are just starting out to get a better understanding of how to build a good credit history. - Learn your rights as a consumer and how to protect them - Learn how to remove negative items from your report (Even the ones you're responsible for) - Correct and remove errors and improve your credit score - Negotiate with creditors to reduce debt - Add positive information to your credit report - Re-Build a Solid Credit history

TAYLOR'S WAY

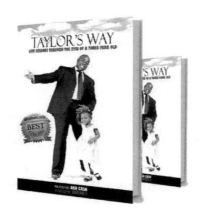

Have you ever spent time observing a child or group of children and how they conduct their young lives? The one thing you will immediately notice is that they live life by their instincts. They are enthusiastic, always eager to learn, curious, brave, and will try almost anything without hesitation. These characteristics and more are all the keys to happiness but unfortunately as we transition from childhood to adulthood we replace these natural instincts with what adults call "reality." As I watched my daughter Taylor grow, I began to realize that she had not been tainted by our ideas of "reality" and as a result was always happy and tended to get everything she wanted out of life effortlessly. Isn't that what we all want of our lives? In the following pages you will read in detail the valuable lessons I've learned from my three year old daughter. Each chapter illustrates through the eyes of a child how you can live a happier life the way it was intended for you to live! Life is abundant! Life is enjoyable! Life is exactly how you imagined it in your wildest dreams! Today is the day that you bring it back to that essence!

MAKING SENSE OF KANYE

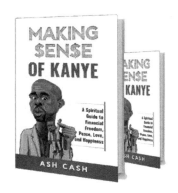

Kanye West has become one of the most controversial artists of the 21st century. His antics often result in the questioning of his sanity and has many people wondering whether he is a master of publicity, who simply knows how to keep his name in the news or if he really needs professional help. Despite that, if we study the man himself and remove emotional reactions from what he says or does, there are many things we can learn from Donda Wests' son. Furthermore, if we take a deeper look into Kanye and his antics, we will see a bigger message as it relates to mental health and money. Making Sense of Kanye is a book designed to teach you how to obtain financial freedom, peace, love, and happiness and how to avoid (or cope with) societal pressures. Using Kanye Wests' misunderstood wisdom, we explore how many of his thoughts coincide with spiritual law and how we can use these laws to live a well-balanced life regardless of economic status. There is no doubt that Mr. West is a musical genius that can sometimes say the wrong things at the wrong time but can we open our minds and allow him to teach us some important aspects of life? This book will show you how!

THE 21 DAY MIND RIGHT, MONEY RIGHT CHALLENGE

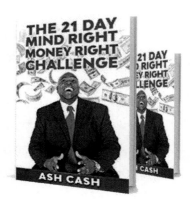

The 21 Day Mind Right, Money Right Challenge is a tool designed to help retrain your brain to effectively attract and attain the financial life you deserve. This is a 21 day challenge that takes you through 21 specific actions so you can renew your money mindset.Get Rid of Old Habits +Learn How Your Old Habits are Keeping You From Your AbundanceCreate Good Vibes Only +Understand the Importance of Clearing Your Mind of Negative ThoughtsChange Your Perspective on Money +Learn and understand that abundance is your birthright and with the right money attitudes you can have everything you want in life Understand The Importance of Meditation with a Quick Start Guide

SCAN QR CODE BELOW TO GO TO

WWW.ASHCASHBOOKS.COM

Ash Cash/Abundance Community Merch Available at
www.AshCashMerch.com

Made in the USA
Columbia, SC
10 January 2022

53986790R00167